Competitive Advantage:

Concepts & Cases

Don Bradmore

Syme Department of Marketing

Monash University

PRENTICE HALL

Sydney   New York   London   Toronto
Tokyo   Singapore   Mexico   Rio de Janeiro

Prentice Hall Australia—Sprint Print is an imprint of Prentice Hall of Australia Pty Ltd. It has been established to provide academics throughout Australia and New Zealand with fast and efficient access to the printing, warehousing and distribution services of Australia's leading educational publisher, ensuring a smooth supply channel to your campus bookseller.

Texts published under the **Prentice Hall Australia—Sprint Print** banner do not undergo the rigorous editorial and development processes normally afforded to Prentice Hall titles. While every effort has been made by the author to ensure the accuracy of the title, Prentice Hall does not take responsibility for the editorial quality of Sprint Print titles.

For more information about the Prentice Hall Australia—Sprint Print service contact the Editorial Department, Prentice Hall Australia, 7 Grosvenor Place, Brookvale, NSW, 2100; Tel. (02)9939 1333.

Special thanks to Amanda Venema of the David Syme Department of Marketing, Monash University, for her fabulous preparation of the manuscript. Her desktop publishing skills and layout of the text were excellent.

© 1996 by Prentice Hall of Australia

All rights reserved. No part of this publication may be reproduced, stored in a retrieval system, or transmitted in any form or by any means, electronic, mechanical, photocopying, recording, or otherwise, without written permission of the publisher.

Acquisitions Editor: Paul Petrulis
Cover design: Jack Jagtenberg

Printed in Australia by Star Printery, Erskineville, NSW

1 2 3 4 5 00 99 98 97 96

ISBN 0 7248 0218 5

Prentice Hall of Australia Pty Ltd, *Sydney*
Prentice Hall, Inc., Englewood Cliffs, *New Jersey*
Prentice Hall International, Inc., *London*
Prentice Hall Canada, Inc., *Toronto*
Prentice Hall Hispanoamericana, *SA, Mexico*
Prentice Hall of India Private Ltd, *New Delhi*
Prentice Hall of Japan, Inc., *Tokyo*
Prentice Hall Southeast Asia Pty Ltd, *Singapore*
Editora Prentice Hall do Brasil Ltda, *Rio de Janeiro*

PRENTICE HALL
A division of Simon & Schuster

Table of Contents

Forward viii

CHAPTER 1:

   THE QUEST FOR COMPETITIVE ADVANTAGE 1

      The Challenge of Change 1

            The Growing Power of Global Competitors 1

            The Increasing Trend Towards Deregulation 2

            The Rapid Pace of Technological Change 2

            Greater Market Fragmentation 2

            Better Educated, More Sophisticated buyers 2

            Greater Protectionism 2

            More Alliances, Acquisitions and Mergers 2

            The Growing Power of Distributors 3

            The rising costs of personal selling 3

            The Declining Effectiveness of the Mass Media 3

      An Age of Unprecedented Competitiveness 3

      Getting a Competitive Edge 4

      Endnotes 5

      When the Going Gets Tough ... : "Gym Wars" 6

      ... The Tough Get Going: "Lauda Wants More" 7

      Case Study 1:   "A Cut-Throat Business: The Fleet Buying
                            Sector of the Australian Motor Industry" 8

      Case Study - Questions for Discussion 11

CHAPTER 2:

THE ECONOMIST'S VIEW OF COMPETITION 13

The Nature of Competition in Different Types of Markets 13

- Pure Competition 13
- Monopolistic Competition 14
- Oligopolistic Competition 15
- Pure Monopoly 16

Significance 18

Limitations 18

When the Going Gets Tough ... : "Trading Hours Reshuffle" 19

... The Tough Get Going: "Bank Bashers" 20

Case Study 2: "Running Out of Puff?" 21

Case Study - Questions for Discussion 24

CHAPTER 3:

COMPETITIVE ADVANTAGE AND THE MARKETING DISCIPLINE 25

In Search of Competitive Advantage: Alternative Orientations or "Mind-Sets" 25

- Production Concept 26
- Product Concept 27
- Selling Concept 27
- Marketing Concept 28
- Societal Marketing Concept 29

Marketing is Competitive Advantage 30

Marketing and Competitive Strategy 30

A New Classification of Competitors 30

- Desire Competitors 31

    Generic Competitors 31

    Product-Form Competitors 31

    Brand Competitors 32

Competitor Analysis 32

    Who Are Our Competitors? 32

    What Are Our Competitors' Objectives? 33

    What Are Our Competitors' Strategies? 33

    What Are Our Competitors' Assumptions? 34

    What Are Our Competitors' Strengths and
    Weaknesses? 34

    What Is Our Competitive Advantage,
    What is Their Competitive Advantage? 34

    What Are Our Competitors' Reaction Patterns? 35

    Which Competitors Should We Attack?
    Which Should We Avoid? 35

    How Can Competitive Intelligence Be Gathered? 35

The Concept of Market Position 36

    The Arthur D. Little Classification 36

    The Ries and Trout Classification 37

    A More Standard Classification 37

        Strategies for the Market Leader 38

        Strategies for the Market Challenger 42

        Strategies for the Market Follower 42

        Strategies for the Market Nicher 42

Insights into Competitive Strategy and Competitive
Advantage from Product Life Cycle Theory 43

    Competitive Turbulence Stage Strategies 44

Endnotes 46

When the Going Gets Tough ... : "Magazine Wars" 47

... The Tough Get Going: "The Battle for the Body" 48

Case Study 3: "Kodak: A New Focus" 49

Case Study - Questions for Discussion 51

CHAPTER 4:

MICHAEL E. PORTER AND SUSTAINABLE COMPETITIVE ADVANTAGE 53

Industry Structure Analysis ("Five Forces" Model) 53

Threat of New Entrants 54
- Economies of Scale 54
- Product Differentiation 54
- Capital Requirements 54
- Cost Disadvantages Regardless of Size 55
- Access to Distribution Barriers 55
- Government Policy 55

Bargaining Power of Buyers 55
Bargaining Power of Suppliers 56
Availability of Substitutes 57
The Intensity of Rivalry 57

The Five Forces Model Illustrated 58

Sources of Sustainable Competitive Advantage - and the Three Generic Strategies 60

The Idea of "Sustainable" Competitive Advantage 61
The Low Cost Advantage 61
The Differentiation Advantage 62
Competitive Scope 64
Three Generic Strategies 65
- Cost Leadership 65
- Differentiation 65
- Focus 66

A Note on Porter's Examples 67
"Stuck-in-the-Middle" 67
Is Being Stuck-in-the-Middle Inevitable? 68
Risks of the Generic Strategies 69

    The Value Chain Concept 69
        Value Activities 70
        Value Activity Labels 71
        Disaggregation of the Value Activities 71

Endnotes 72

When the Going Gets Tough ... : "Aspirin Wars" 74

... The Tough Get Going: "The Biker Brigade: A Niche Player in a Big Market" 75

Case Study 4: "Woolworths Sizes Up Its Great Competitor" 76

Case Study - Questions for Discussion 78

CHAPTER 5:

THE "NEW WISDOM" OF ROSABETH MOSS KANTER 79

New Wisdom 79

Core Competence 80

Time Compression 81

Continuous Improvement 83

Relationships 85

The Importance of Social Factors 87

Endnotes 88

When the Going Gets Tough ... : "Petrol Wars" 89

... The Tough Get Going: "Whitegoods Wars" 90

Case Study 5: "Spotlight's Competitive Edge" 91

Case Study - Questions for Discussion 93

CHAPTER 6:

THE BATTLEFIELD OF THE MARKETPLACE: SPECIFIC WEAPONS OF WAR 95

- War in the Marketplace 95
- Some Weapons of War 95
    - Corporate Capabilities 96
    - Flexible Manufacturing 96
    - Cost Flexibility 96
    - Information Techology 97
    - Total Quality Management 97
    - Superior Customer Service 97
    - Benchmarking 98
    - Strategic Alliances 99
    - Innovation 99
- The Armoury Extended 100
    - Logistics Management 100
    - Relationship Marketing 100
    - Competitive Advantage Through People 101
    - Brand Building 101
    - Direct Marketing 101
    - Business Process Re-engineering 102
    - Marketing Implementation 102
- Corporate Restructuring 103
- Endnotes 104
- When the Going Gets Tough ... : "Rugby Wars" 105
- ... The Tough Get Going: "A Transport Juggernaut Drives the Benefits of a Rejig" 106
- Case Study 6: "The Times They Are A-Changing" 107
- Case Study - Questions for Discussion 109

CHAPTER 7:

THE ABILITY TO COMPETE 111

Determinants of Competitive Success 111

Opportunities for Competitive Advantage 112

Assessing Competitive Advantage 113

The Day & Wensley Framework for Assessing Competitive Advantage 115

Identification of Key Success Factors 115

Assessment of the Sources of Advantage 116

Assessment of Positional Advantage 116

Assessment of Performance Outcomes 117

Competitor-Centered and Customer-Centered Measures of Competitive Advantage 117

Methods for Assessing Sources of Advantage or Distinctive Competences 117

Methods for Assessing Positional Advantage 118

Methods for Assessing Key Success Factors 119

Methods for Assessing Measures of Performance 120

Evolving Company Orientations 122

Endnotes 122

When the Going Gets Tough ... : "Hoping for a Stylish Success" 123

... The Tough Get Going: "Oil and Coal Wars" 124

Case Study 7:   "'Bad'" Ideas That Win in an Age of Hypercompetition" 125

Case Study - Questions for Discussion 127

Bibliography 129

Foreword

We live in an age of unprecedented competitiveness.

While some Asian economies have experienced spectacular growth in the decade of the Nineties, those of most of the Western world have struggled to recover from the recessed state into which they fell in the late Eighties.

Most economic analysts predict that unemployment levels are likely to remain high into the foreseeable future, and that whatever growth can be expected will be low and slow. As a result, there are global gluts of wool, wheat, meat and other agricultural products, chemicals, steel, automobiles and many other goods and services. As Philip Kotler puts it in the Preface to his *Marketing Management: Analysis, Planning, Implementation and Control* (seventh edition, 1991), "throughout the world there are simply too many products chasing too few customers."

But, as Kotler again points out, weak economies are not the only problem. Today, businesses of all kinds face many other serious challenges: the growing power of global competitors, an increasing trend towards deregulation, the rapid pace of technological change, greater market fragmentation, more sophisticated and discerning buyers, the declining effectiveness of mass media, and many more.

All of these challenges have led inevitably to an intensification of competition.

Today's business leaders must look for new ways to survive, to prosper and to grow. In short, they need a "competitive edge".

But how can a "competitive edge" be developed?

More importantly, perhaps, what are the "issues" upon which success will depend in an increasingly dynamic and hostile environment?

There are no simple answers to questions such as these.

What constitutes a competitive edge in one industry does not constitute it in another. The issues that are relevant today will not necessarily be those that are relevant tomorrow.

Nevertheless, an attempt must be made to find the answers. In tracing the major lines of development in the thinking about how to compete in business, in roughly chronological order, this book is intended to provide a starting point.

The Quest for Competitive Advantage

Business enterprises of all kinds are created for one purpose - to achieve the goals and objectives of their stakeholders. In the case of most businesses, the primary goal is to make profits.

Some enterprises, usually referred to as non-profit organisations, have other primary goals, such as the provision of charitable works (the Salvation Army and the Red Cross, for instance), or the pursuit of political office (the Australian Labor Party, the Liberal Party of Australia), or success on the sporting field (the Australian Cricket Board, the Collingwood Football Club). Even for organisations such as these, however, profits (or surpluses) are usually necessary if they are to survive to carry on their work.

All enterprises, whether oriented to the pursuit of profit or to the pursuit of any other goal, compete with each other - to a greater of lesser extent - for the patronage of customers. Those which exist to make profits compete for our time and attention, seeking to extract from us the money which we have to spend or invest. Those which exist for non-profit motives also compete for our time and attention, and, as we have seen, often for our money as well.

In the Fabulous Fifties and Soaring Sixties, as the U.S. academic Philip Kotler has noted, companies could reasonably ignore their competitors. In those post-war boom decades, there was sufficient growth in the economies of the world for all competitors to achieve realistic growth targets. However, as economic conditions worsened in the Turbulent Seventies and Flat Eighties, achieving satisfactory levels of company growth increasingly depended on the ability of firms to wrest market share from competitors. Companies had little choice but to cultivate competitiveness.[1]

The Challenge of Change

While some of the economies of Asia have experienced spectacular growth in the decade of Nineties, those of the Western world have struggled to recover from the recessed state into which they fell in the late eighties. Most economic analysts predict that unemployment levels are likely to remain high into the foreseeable future and what growth can be expected will be low and slow. As a result, there are global gluts of wool, meat and other agricultural produce, minerals, steel, automobiles and many other goods and services. As Philip Kotler puts it, there are simply "too many products chasing too few customers".[2]

But weak economies are not the only problem. Businesses today face many other serious challenges. These include:

The growing power of global competitors

Large, global competitors, with major economies of scale, threaten the viability of many local producers. Well-resourced, and with products such as cars, photocopying machines, toys, electrical goods and so on that are well suited to global marketing, they can offer high quality goods and services at low cost. They also threaten the viability of local companies which sell their goods and services to local producers or buy goods and services from them.

The increasing trend towards deregulation

Governments in many countries are deregulating their industries, opening them up to market forces in an effort to improve their international competitiveness. While this represents a relaxation of government control of industries, a paradoxical tightening of government control in other areas of business increases the difficulty of competing for many. Today, business leaders are speaking out against the burden of reporting and the volume of paperwork imposed by new government legislation. Pressure groups (such as labor unions and the consumer movement) and ethical, social and environmental concerns often exacerbate the difficulty of remaining competitive.

The rapid pace of technological change

The pace of technological change has never been more rapid. To remain competitive (and even to survive), many businesses are constantly faced with the need to acquire new, more complex and more expensive manufacturing and support technology. Moreover, as product life-cycles shorten, more new products, more technologically complex products and more frequent new product introductions are becoming necessary.

Greater market fragmentation

Markets are fragmenting. As Regis McKenna puts it: "Technology is transforming choice, and choice is transforming the marketplace."[3] What he implies is that the days of mass marketing are over. Today's greater diversity of consumer needs and wants means smaller market segments and that calls for smaller, often more costly, production runs. As one prominent Australian marketing consultant has recently observed, "The difficulty today is not in finding segments in the market, but in finding markets in the segments."

Better educated, more sophisticated buyers

Today's consumers are more discerning than ever before. Better educated, more sophisticated, they show less brand loyalty, less store loyalty and less supplier loyalty. They are prepared to shop around and have a much greater concern with price. Similarly, better educated and better trained professional buyers are proving harder for manufacturers and their representatives to deal with than at any time in the past.

Greater protectionism

While many governments around the world deregulate their industries, opening them up to competition in an attempt to improve their competitiveness, other governments continue to protect their industries, building tariff barriers to protect them from imports. They continue to subsidise their local industries to inhibit competition from abroad; they actively support price-cutting in foreign markets. All of these conditions make the going difficult for local firms striving to compete in world markets.

More alliances, acquisitions and mergers

Through takeovers, acquisitions and mergers and more powerful through joint ventures and other alliances; the big get bigger while the small often get less competitive. However, even for large

Chapter 1: The Quest For Competitive Advantage

firms, alliances, mergers and takeovers can present problems. While they are often the solution to company difficulties, they may distract managers who must come to grips quickly with new products, new customers and new priorities.

The growing power of distributors

In many industries, the growing bargaining power of distributors is having the effect of eroding the profitability of manufacturers. In many instances, they are faced with a quest for alternative distribution methods in order to survive.

The rising costs of personal selling

As selling costs rise, many manufacturers are searching for alternatives - in direct marketing, sponsorship, telemarketing, etc. - as they attempt to attract and retain a customer base of adequate size.

The declining effectiveness of mass media

The traditional mass communication channels - television, radio and print advertising, in particular - are declining in effectiveness. Breaking through the "clutter" presents severe difficulties for many producers and distributors.

An Age of Unprecedented Competitiveness

In the face of these many challenges, all of which lead inevitability to an intensification of competition, business leaders are constantly looking for new ways to compete. They are continually searching for the issues upon which their competitive success will depend. They are looking for the "competitive edge" they need to survive, to prosper and to grow.

But, how can a competitive edge to be developed? What are the issues upon which success depends in such a hostile, dynamic and competitive environment?

One approach to an answer to these critical questions has been provided by David W. Cravens, Professor of Marketing at the Texas Christian University, Fort Worth, Texas. His research has revealed that there are at least five essential criteria for success in "this age of unprecedented competitiveness":

i. **The ability to recognise that these are troubled and volatile times.**

    As markets are deregulated to allow for greater competition, as well-resourced global competitors enter once protected markets and as rapid technological advances are made in industries of all types, those business enterprises led by managers who cannot accept that the times are changing will inevitably fail. "Complacency," he reminded his audience, "is the forerunner to disaster."

ii. **The ability to get closer to customers.**

    Getting closer to customers means knowing what customers mean by "value" and what they are prepared to pay for it. To some, value may mean quality; to others, it may mean features,

Competitive Advantage: Concepts and Cases

or service, or price, or convenience, or some other thing. The point is that the purchase decisions of customers' will certainly be made in terms of their perceptions of the relative value of the offerings of competitors. Firms which do not know what their customers' perceptions of value are, are also destined to failure.

iii. **The ability to formulate sound strategies for competing successfully.**

This calls for the ability to analyse competitors' objectives and strategies as well as that of formulating strategies to attract and retain a customer base of an appropriate size.

iv. **The ability to choose wisely which markets to enter and, more importantly perhaps, which not to enter.**

This requires a sound understanding of the company's own resources and capabilities, and of its strengths and weaknesses, opportunities and threats. It calls for a sound knowledge of the key success factors for each targeted segment. It calls for a sound appreciation of market conditions and trends.

v. **The ability to implement programs that deliver the needs and wants of customers in the targeted segments more precisely than those of competitors.**

It is one thing to know what is required for marketplace success but quite another thing to implement programs that deliver it. High order skills in planning, organising, communicating and relating are required to ensure that which is delivered precisely matches that which was promised.[4]

Getting a Competitive Edge

While few would deny the soundness of Cravens' advice, some might seek more detailed prescriptions for implementing it. How, exactly, does a firm get "closer" to its customers? What makes a strategy "sound"? Are techniques available to guide an organisation in its selection of the market segments to enter and avoid? And, assuming that a firm does develop and implement sound strategies, what can give it a "competitive edge" over other firms whose strategies are equally well formulated and implemented?

There are no simple answers to these questions. But, the chapters which follow are intended to provide a starting point for the thinking of those whose task it is to guide the firm in its attempt to maintain and improve its ability to compete.

In Chapter 2, we look specifically at traditional approaches to competition, focusing our attention on the way in which economists have long considered its nature.

In Chapter 3, we examine contributions to the study of competition from the formal discipline of marketing. First, we explore the way in which the economist's definition of competitors was found wanting when marketing emerged as the dominant managerial philosophy in the post-Great Depression, post-World War II days of the late forties and early fifties. We examine the adoption by organisations of the marketing philosophy as a means in itself to competitive advantage. We examine particular aspects of marketing theory which seem to provide insights into approaches to the

Chapter 1: The Quest For Competitive Advantage

formulation of competitive marketing strategy, focusing especially on competitive analysis, market position strategies, and product life-cycle theory.

Chapter 4 is devoted to the work of Harvard's Michael E. Porter, whose contributions when they appeared in the early and mid 1980s had an effect on business thinking about competitiveness which can only be described as "explosive". His industry structure model, his generic strategies for competitive advantage and his value chain concept, all of which have had their share of criticism, have held sway in this field of study for more than a decade. It is fair to say that he has had more influence on competitive strategy formulation and the concept of competitive advantage than any other person before or since.

In Chapter 5, we examine some more recent views on how to compete effectively in business, views brought to the attention of an eager readership by Rosabeth Moss Kanter in the early 1990s in her (then) role as editor of the Harvard Business Review. Very clearly, the "new wisdom" she espoused indicates the way forward.

Chapter 6 deals with some other issues which are seen to be significant today by many organisations as they strive to gain and maintain a competitive edge.

We conclude in Chapter 7 with an approach to the way in which an organisation can assess its ability to compete more effectively. In this sense, the chapter summarises what has gone before, integrating the material cohesively.

Endnotes

1. See Preface in Philip Kotler, *Marketing Management: Analysis, Planning, Implementation and Control*, Prentice Hall, Englewood Cliffs, seventh edition, 1991.

2. ibid.

3. "Marketing is Everything", *Harvard Business Review*, September/October, 1992.

4. From a lecture given by David W. Cravens at Monash University, May 1992.

WHEN THE GOING GETS TOUGH ...

GYM WARS

Feeling unfit? It's your lucky day. As the fitness industry sharpens its competitive edge, Melbourne gyms are cutting membership fees in half, or giving away sports shoes, mobile phones and air tickets to entice new members.

In central Melbourne, where there are 50 fitness centres in a five-kilometre square, gyms are caught in a spiralling discounting war. The membership scramble has been fuelled by a spate of gym closures. At least a dozen of Melbourne's 250 gyms, including the once-exclusive Ultimate, off Toorak Road, have collapsed in the past year. In the past two weeks, two gyms - Just Aerobics and Fitness Edge - have shut, leaving about 1200 members out of pocket. The best they can hope for is a discounted rate at another gym.

The Victorian Fitness Industry Association (VFIA), which has 50 members, wants to set up an indemnity fund to compensate people who are left high and dry by gym closures. At present, consumers can make a complaint to the Office of Fair Trading, but they are not entitled to compensation.

According to the president of the VFIA, Mr Nathan Shafir, about 4 per cent of Victorians now hold gym memberships - a figure that is slightly lower than it was twenty years ago. "A lot more people are doing sport, jogging or walking, and so don't belong to gyms now," he said.

Another industry spokesperson believes that Victoria has reached saturation point in "off-the-rack" fitness. "People are getting a little sick of the traditional gym membership. But there is a big growth in personal training," he said.

The gyms, which charge between $299 and $1300 for a year's membership, are competing for a very fussy market, one which is largely dominated by women. To keep up their appeal, most gyms have been discounting heavily. On offer were mobile phones, holidays in Noumea, pairs of sneakers, two-for-one memberships and scratch-and-win tickets.

Once people had joined, they expected more for their money than barbells and stomach crunches. At the $1300 a year Re-Creation in Armadale, there is a creche, jacuzzi, and "cardio theatre" where members can ride an electric bicycle, watch movies or listen to their favourite CDs. Last year, the centre offered new members a $495 Motorola mobile phone.

In contrast, Zaks, in neighbouring Prahran, offers full membership for $299 (cut from $499). "Hundreds of people have taken it up," said the marketing director. The owner of the Equinox, also in Prahran, said his gym offered cut-price membership of $40 a month for customers from other gyms that had gone broke, but, in general, did not give discounts. It did have membership drives, however. The most recent was a mail-out to 100,000 homes of cards showing Mr Kemp cuddling Elle Macpherson.

(Source: Adapted from "Gym Wars", an article by Rachel Buchanan, Age, 2 September 1994.)

Chapter 1: The Quest For Competitive Advantage

... THE TOUGH GET GOING

LAUDA WANTS MORE

Lauda Air is gearing up for the departure of Lufthansa from the Australian aviation market later this year, pushing for more flights and planning to set up its own reservations, sales and marketing divisions in Australia.

The Austrian-based Lauda is keen to develop a long-term business strategy in Australia, effectively going it alone, as Lufthansa prepares to abandon flights to Australia in six months time.

Lufthansa, which has a 39 per cent stake in Lauda, now provides the reservations and sales network for Lauda in Australia. Lufthansa, which had originally planned to dump its flights to Australia next month after 30 years of service to the region, has decided to keep up its flights, even though they are unprofitable, until the end of September.

Lauda's commercial director, Mr Derek Jewson, said the airline would set up its own sales, marketing and reservations units in Australia as soon as possible. "We will naturally continue our close association with Lufthansa in Australia and cooperate with them where it makes commercial sense to do so," he said. "We have invested considerable time and effort into the Australian operation, which is now profitable."

Lauda flies Boeing 767-300 aircraft from Melbourne to Vienna, via Singapore, twice a week. It hopes to build this service to four flights a week.

Lufthansa is working towards a joint agreement with Thai Airways to fly passengers from Frankfurt to Australia via Bangkok. Talks are continuing between the two carriers.

Lufthansa operates three services a week to Sydney.

(Adapted from an article by Bruce Tobin, "Lauda Wants More Flights", *Age*, 6 February 1995, p.24.)

CASE STUDY 1:

A CUT-THROAT BUSINESS: THE FLEET BUYING SECTOR OF THE AUSTRALIAN MOTOR INDUSTRY

The earliest barometer of this nation's economic health is not the housing and construction industry, but the automotive industry. With its finely tuned antennas, business is the first to sense a decline and one of its first moves is to freeze any expenditure that can be postponed. And the most immediate of these is generally the car fleet.

Fleet buying - both business and government - is the mainstay of the Australian motor industry. Two out of every three cars sold in Australia today goes into a fleet. The big six-cylinder Falcons and Commodores sell about 75 per cent into fleet life. So, when a company, big or small, decides to hold on to its vehicles until the economy starts to improve, its immediately reflected in the market.

That's what's caused fleet sales to plummet into a three-year trough that ended only last year when they increased by 11 per cent to over 616,000 sales, the fifth-best year on record. However, the fleets came back into the market earlier than the private buyers to be the first to leave, predicting a new-vehicle sales increase this year of only 2.5 to 3 per cent.

Observers believe private buyers will be quick to zip up their wallets, because of high interest rates and the probability of further rises, the expectations of a tough federal Budget, two state elections this year, and the uncertainty of Canberra's manoeuvring towards the next federal poll.

In fact, fleet buying still hasn't caught up. Australia's biggest fleet management company, Fleet Systems, with 96,000 vehicles on its computer data base, says that in 1989 the average mileage of a fleet vehicle being traded in on a new car was just under 90,000 kilometres. From then on it climbed steeply as fleets postponed their changeover decisions, rising to 115,000 average in mid-1992.

It has since started to drop, but still hovers around 102,000 kilometres. The company's chief executive, David Stockley, says the car industry will have to wait for a year or two yet before trade-in points return to pre-recession figures.

Most of the cars bought by both private and government fleets are Australian-built. Even now there is pressure on governments and, more indirectly, on business, to buy Australian for their fleets. Toyota Australia exploded in anger last year when it discovered that three Federal Government departments were examining the feasibility of buying small cars from Korea, Japan and Spain, from the $14,000 to $18,000 price bracket.

This was because the new locally made Corolla had gone up in size and to a baseline recommended retail price of $23,000. Faced with the possibility of losing 6,000 Corolla sales

Chapter 1: The Quest For Competitive Advantage

a year, Toyota Australia was quick to remind Canberra just who had spent $420-odd million on a new assembly plant at Altona.

The cars bought by fleets are Ford Falcon, Holden Commodore, Mitsubishi Magna/Verada, Toyota Camry/Vienta and the Corolla. The local prestige cars, Holden's Statesman/Caprice, Ford's Fairlane/LTD, also dominate fleet luxury car sales - Prime Minister Paul Keating rides in a Caprice.

The dealers don't particularly like it because the factories shut them out of deals direct with clients, including fleet management companies and finance houses, leaving the retailer only the profit involved in future servicing and parts and whatever profit is in the trade-ins.

The big four car makers have tuned the fleet market into a cut-throat business. They chase every sale, cutting prices to the bone to make deals, stealing business from each other, to the point where there are grounds for believing they may even be losing money on fleet business and making it only on private buyers.

Discounted prices and lower operating costs are the bottom line for most fleet buyers to favour the local cars. Fleet Systems has just produced figures covering 23,000 vehicles from its data bank, automatic petrol-engined sedans having covered 65,000-95,000 kilometres, showing average fuel consumption figures and costs per 1000 kilometres of service, repairs, tyres and similar.

The VR Commodore Berlina and the V6 Toyota Vienta both return the lowest running costs of $19 per 1000 kilometres, with the VR Commodore next on $22, Camry four-cylinder $24, Magna four $25, and ED Falcon GLi $26. By comparison, the imported Mazda 626 and Honda Accord 2.2-litre fours cost $36 per 1000 kilometres.

The big sixes were even cheaper than what we once regarded as small cars - another reason why they dominate the market. The Fleet Systems figures show the Corolla costing $27 per 1000 kilometres to maintain and the previous Ford Laser $28.

Their only advantage is in fuel consumption figures, for they get just on 10 litres per 100 kilometres where the Commodore averaged 10.7 and the Falcon 11.4. There's an interesting comparison with the big cars: the Fleet Systems figures show the Ford Fairlane Ghia V8 returning 14.8 litres per 100 kilometres and $39 per 1000 kilometres to maintain while the Holden Statesman V8 returns only 15.8 litres per 100 kilometres and costs $41 per 1000 kilometres to maintain.

However, while the imported cars are certainly up against it when it comes to fleet discount prices, spare parts costs and maintenance, one must never forget that the Big Four in Australia (Ford, Holden, Toyota and Mitsubishi) are importers as well as local builders. Ford sources its Festiva from Korea; Holden sources its from Spain; Mitsubishi sources its Lancers from Japan. All are in there to take advantage of the way in which Toyota (with the Corolla) and Ford (with the Laser) have vacated the small car segment.

Hard on their heels are Hyundai Excel, with a prestigious reputation for durability and running costs, the new Daewoo, cheap and tough, and, since last January, the Spanish-built Seat (with three models - Ibiza, Cordoba and Toleda - starting at $16,200.)

It's a tough game, this fleet business, and it's being made more complex by the shifting sands of interest rates. These are responsible for the growing number of extraordinarily attractive offers in recent times by car makers' in-house finance arms and independent brokers to fleet buyers. Typical of these are Holden's SmartBuy (a no-deposit, guaranteed buy-back program) and Hertz's offer of new car leases on late-model used cars.

(Adapted from an article by Bill Tuckey, "New Car Sales Slow To Recover Despite Cut-throat Pricing", *Age*, 2 March 1995. p.25.)

Chapter 1: The Quest For Competitive Advantage

CASE STUDY - QUESTIONS FOR DISCUSSION

1. How have the recessed economic conditions in Australia in recent years affected the fleet buying segment of the automobile industry?

2. To what extent do you agree with the writer of this article that business "with its finely tuned antennas" is the first to sense a decline in the economy?

3. Do you think Toyota Australia's anger was justified when it discovered last year that some Federal Government departments were considering importing small cars for their employees from Korea, Spain and Japan? Give your reasons.

4. In what ways, if at all, has the availability of low-priced, high-quality imported cars (from Korea and Spain, in particular) affected the ability of the local Australian car manufacturers to compete?

5. What evidence, if any, can you find in this case to suggest that local car manufacturers are attempting to get "closer" to their customers (in the way described by Dr David W. Cravens)?

6. Discuss this sentence from the case: "The dealers don't particularly like it because the factories shut them out of deals direct with clients, including fleet management companies and finance houses ... " What does this say about the bargaining power of dealers in the Australian car industry? How has deregulation of the automobile industry impacted on the dealers (as opposed to the car manufacturers?.)

7. Discuss the implications of the "Big Four" car makers in Australia turning the fleet market into "a cut-throat business"? Is there really anything wrong with the local car manufacturers stealing business from each other by "cutting prices to the bone"?

8. Explain the sentence, "Discounted prices and lower operating costs are the bottom line for most fleet buyers to favour the local cars". What are the implications of this for local car manufacturers?

9. Discuss the implications for local car manufacturers of a large firm (such as Fleet Systems) having a data bank of the running costs of various vehicle makes and models. In what circumstances can a local car manufacturer whose vehicle does not fare particularly well in the figures (as compiled by Fleet Systems in this case) compete successfully in the fleet segment of the market? [Note that the Holden Statesman V8, for example, does not rate well in terms of petrol economy and maintenance costs.]

10. Towards the end of the case, the writer says, "It's a tough game the fleet segment, and it's being made tougher by the shifting sands of interest rates." Do you agree that "It's a tough game"? To what extent do you agree that it is "being made more complex by the shifting sands of interest rates"? What are the local car manufacturers doing to address this problem? How would you assess the soundness of their strategy? Is there an alternative (or better) strategy?

Competitive Advantage: Concepts and Cases

CHAPTER 2

The Economist's View of Competition

In the previous chapter the point was made that it is surprising that not more has been written about how to compete. After all, competition has always been a fact of business life.

Until relatively recently, most of what was written about the competitive situation within markets came from the discipline of economics. For the economist, the prime focus of interest in this regard was the varying latitudes to pricing which different competitive conditions imply.

The Nature of Competition in Different Types of Markets

Traditionally, the economist's assessment of the intensity of competition in a particular market has been based on the number of companies operating within it; that is, the more sellers, the greater the competition.

For the economist, depending on the number of competitors, four market structures exist: pure competition, monopolistic competition, oligopolistic competition and pure monopoly.

Pure Competition

Pure competition exists where there are an infinite number of sellers of a product which is homogeneous (or virtually identical).

Being unable to perceive differences in the products of the sellers, buyers are easily able to substitute one seller's product for another's. As no one seller has any more, or any less, power or control over the market than any other seller, the degree of concentration can be said to be zero. (See Figure 2.1 which summarises the important dimensions of each market type.)

There are no barriers to entry. Any new seller may enter the market at will. Similarly, there are no barriers to exit. Sellers are free to exit the market at any time. In the terms of the economist, this characteristic is referred to as "high mobility of resources"; there are no financial barriers to coming into, or leaving, the market.

All sellers have perfect market information. No seller has any advantage of knowledge (or information about market conditions) which is not available to all other sellers. Similarly, all buyers have perfect market knowledge.

Because the product of all sellers is virtually the same, no seller will charge more for the product than any other seller. If any seller did attempt to set a higher price than other sellers, he or she would make no sales at all because the buyers can buy all the product they require at the lower price. Nor

Competitive Advantage: Concepts and Cases

would any seller attempt to charge less than the price charged by other sellers because all sellers can sell as much as they wish at the market price. Thus, in markets characterised by pure competition, sellers are referred to as "price takers" rather than "price makers".

As there is an infinite number of sellers, each competitor controls a very small percentage of the market.

Under these conditions, there is no advantage to be gained by individual sellers from any form of non-price competition - building a stronger sales team than competitors, or spending more on advertising and sales promotion, for instance. Because the product is homogeneous, because the sellers can sell all they can produce at the market price, and because the buyers have perfect market knowledge, expenditure on promotion of this type is not justified.

Nor is any other form of marketing expenditure justified. Marketing research is unjustified; new product development is unjustified; marketing strategy formulation is unjustified.

From all of this, however, it is obvious that the market type which the economist refers to as "pure competition" cannot ever exist; the concept is a theoretical one only.

Commodity markets, such as those in which minerals, timber, fish, wool, grains, fruit and other primary produce are sold, provide the closest examples of markets in which something approaching pure competition might be seen to exist.

Although pure competition exists only in theory, economists have found the construct useful. It provides insights into market conditions and market operations which help to explain economic phenomena in the real world.

Monopolistic Competition

Monopolistic competition exists where there are many sellers and many buyers of a products which are similar, but not identical, to others on offer. By defining their market very narrowly, sellers in this type of market could be said to have 100 per cent of it.

Each seller in this market type is able to differentiate the product to some degree - by features, quality or style; by product formulation or brand or packaging; by price or distribution method; by the extra services (such as repairs, maintenance and warranty) which a manufacturer can add, and so on.

Thus, the products of sellers in this market type are perceived to be different by buyers. As a result, buyers are prepared to pay a higher price for products which they perceive to offer more value to them. Price competition and non-price competition are both common, and important. Sellers who can create value in their products in the eyes, minds and hearts of buyers can earn above-average profits. For this reason, many competitors will try to build strong barriers to entry by means such as the building of their brand strength, the acquisition of patents and licences, and the investment in expensive manufacturing technology.

Chapter 2: The Economist's View of Competition

It should be noted that these same factors can also create barriers to exit. In markets of monopolistic competition, a player can be locked into a segment that it would prefer not to be in, because it has invested so heavily in it that it cannot simply walk away when a down-turn in the market occurs.

In markets of this type, too, sellers will attempt to raise the switching costs of buyers, attempting to lock them in to their product. For example, a computer manufacturer might produce its own software packages for use exclusively with its machines. Having bought the machines, the customer may be reluctant to switch to another make when considering a new purchase because that would also mean the purchase of more new software.

Markets characterised by monopolistic competition are those which are most familiar to us as consumers. In the markets for such products as clothing and footwear, breakfast cereals, furniture and so on, each producer can be said to have a monopoly of a kind over its own product. Each is able to differentiate it by brand name, features and options, packaging materials, service levels, and the like.

In such markets, sellers are highly sensitive to the competitive strategies of others. Because there are (theoretically at least) many sellers, each seller is less affected by the competitive strategies of others than is the case in the oligopoly market types which we will now consider.

Oligopolistic Competition

Oligopolistic competition exists where there are only a few large sellers of a product.

Oligopolistic markets are of two types; differentiated and undifferentiated. In differentiated oligopolies, a fair degree of product uniqueness may exist; in undifferentiated oligopolies, little product differentiation is possible.

Instances of differentiated oligopolies are not difficult to find in Australian industry. The "Big Four" banks - the Commonwealth Bank, the National Australia Bank, the Westpac Banking Corporation and the ANZ Bank dominate the industry; the "Big Four" car manufacturers - The Ford Motor Company, Holden Motors, Toyota Australia and Mitsubishi Australia dominate the Australian automobile industry. Qantas Airways and Australian Airlines dominate the Australian domestic airline industry. Telecom Australia and Optus dominate the Australian telecommunications industry. Other examples may spring to mind in regard to the oil industry, the television broadcasting industry, the radio broadcasting industry, the newspaper and magazine industry, and so on. While the competitors in all of these industries have products that are broadly similar (in that one can reasonably be substituted for the other), they are able to differentiate them to a good degree. Buyers of their products are able to perceive that one organisation's product offers more value to them than another's.

Instances of undifferentiated oligopolies are more difficult to identify, and yet many exist. In industries in which there are only a few manufacturers of products such as crushed rock, cement, concrete pipes, timber products, newsprint and other paper and cardboard products, some forms of plastic and the like, undifferentiated oligopolies abound. For manufacturers of products of this type, little product uniqueness is possible. Some opportunity for differentiation may exist, of course, in regard to promotion and distribution.

While there may be quite a number of sellers in both forms of oligopoly markets (differentiated and undifferentiated), these markets are dominated by a few "giant" sellers - because the entry barriers, often in the form of capital requirements, patents, control over raw materials, scarce locations, or some combination of these, are high. The relative fewness of significant competitors means that each of them has a large share of the market.

In this oligopolistic industries, there is an extraordinary sensitivity among the large sellers to the marketing strategies and tactics of the others. This is particularly so in regard to pricing strategy. If one major seller, for instance, reduces the price of its product, even minimally, there can be massive shifts in market share, with all the difficulties that implies for every other major competitor. Hence, in oligopoly markets, a price reduction by one big firm usually means that every other major player will follow suit (or increase its services to compensate); if it does not, it risks losing customers to the low price competitor. On the other hand, if one seller increases its price, other sellers will not necessarily emulate it, and again this can have far-reaching effects.

Thus, because an oligopolist can never be sure what will happen if it reduces or increases its price, competition on price is generally avoided. Not surprisingly, non-price competition is often intense.

In this sense, oligopoly markets usually provide the keenest competitive battles of all. Each seller must be constantly alert, and ready to react, to every other competitor's moves.

Pure Monopoly

Pure monopoly exists where there is one seller only. Because the monopolist is the only seller, the product has high uniqueness and there are no easy substitutes.

Often, the monopolist is a government instrumentality. Telecom Australia still has a virtual monopoly over the provision of domestic telephone services; Australia Post still has a monopoly over delivery of householder mail. Melbourne Water, the State Electricity Commission of Victoria and various other government utilities enjoy a monopoly position in their respective markets.

Sometimes, the monopolist is a private regulated monopoly. That is, the enterprise is owned by its shareholders but its activities, because they affect big numbers of the community, are constrained by government. British Telecom is a private regulated monopoly. If the Victorian Government floats its State Electricity Commission (as it proposes to do) and still maintains some manner of control, it will be a private regulated monopoly.

Less frequently, the seller is a private unregulated monopoly. BHP has a monopoly in some sectors of the steel industry in Australia, for example.

In each of these situations, pricing strategy is handled differently. In government monopolies, there may be many objectives. The government may choose to set low prices, running its monopoly at a loss in the public interest. It may set prices to generate revenues. In private regulated monopolies the government usually allows the board of management to set a "fair" price, but one that enables the business to maintain and develop its capacity. In private unregulated monopolies, the business may set whatever price it chooses, but, often fearful of attracting unfavourable attention of governments, it will usually set a price geared more to market penetration than to profit maximisation.

Chapter 2: The Economist's View of Competition

Non-price strategies and tactics (personal selling, sales promotion, sponsorship and advertising, etc,) are usually important, not to wrest market share from direct competitors (because there are none) but to expand the total market.

Fig. 2.1: Important Dimensions of Each Market Type

Important Dimensions	Pure Competition	Monopolistic Competition	Oligopolistic Competition	Pure Monopoly
No. of Sellers	Infinite	Many	Few	One
Size of Sellers	Small	Small to Large	Large	Large
Degree of Concentration (Ratio: 0-100)	0	50	75	100
Product Differentiation	Undifferentiated	Differentiated	Differentiated or Undifferentiated	Unique
Barriers to Entry and Exit	None	Low to High	High	High
Control of Price by Firm	None	High	High	Total but constraints
Importance of Price Competition	None	Important	Usually	None
Importance of Non-Price Competition	None	High	High	None but used to expand total market

Significance

The important dimensions of market behaviour discussed above, and summarised in Figure 2.1, have long been of interest to economists. Their set of analytical tools have been found useful in defining and understanding the behaviour of the firms which compete in different market types, and that of their customers.

Perhaps the most significant aspect of this, for business practitioners at least, is what it implies about the use of price as a competitive weapon. As most markets in Australia can be categorised, in economic terms, as either forms of monopolistic competition or forms of oligopolistic competition (where, as we have seen, pricing is most critical), the efficacy of price as a competitive weapon is worth further brief consideration.

How effective price is competition is in each of these industry types will ultimately depend on the financial and marketing strength of the industry rivals. However, if one company's manufacturing, marketing and distribution costs are significantly lower than a competitor's, price can be a powerful weapon; the low-cost seller can withstand a price war with considerably less threat to its survival than a high-cost seller.

Nevertheless, it is generally agreed that price reductions are not the most effective way for one competitor to counter another. Unless the market share of the firm which initiates the price cut increases, the net result may simply be a reduction in its profits.

Successful pricing strategy depends on the skilful analysis of competitors' objectives, resources and capabilities, and this includes the anticipation of their likely response to competitors' pricing initiatives. We will discuss the need for, and the content of, this analysis in Chapter 3.

Limitations

We started this work in Chapter 1 with the thought that every firm is - to some degree at least - in competition with every other firm. All firms, profit and non-profit alike, compete for the time, attention and money of the customer groups they target.

While the economist's view of competitive structures has provided many valuable insights for business practitioners, it fails to account for the fact that firms in any market face competition from firms outside their industries as well as from those within it.

For this reason, as we shall see when we turn our attention to the marketing discipline in Chapter 3, the economist's view of competitive structures was quickly rejected when the new "science" of marketing began to emerge in the period after the Second World War.

Chapter 2: The Economist's View of Competition

WHEN THE GOING GETS TOUGH ...

TRADING HOURS RESHUFFLE

Retail and general business groups have urged the State Government of Victoria to simplify Sunday trading laws. They want the first Sunday of each month as a trading day.

However, both groups are at odds with the total deregulation of trading hours, an idea being pushed by the Victorian Employers Chamber of Commerce and Industry.

The Executive Officer of the Combined Retailers Association of Victoria, Mr Tony Christakakis, said Sunday trading dates should be standardised, but he believed that total deregulation of trading hours was not economically sustainable and would harm many small businesses.

The Deputy Director of the Retail Traders Association of Victoria, Mr Wayne Gannon, agreed. He also called for the simplification of Sunday trading laws, saying that they should reflect "the special needs of various industry sectors and geographic locations".

But Mr Ian Smith, a spokesperson for the Minister for Small Business, Mr Heffernan, has said that the Government has no plans to change the Sunday trading laws at present. He rejected the suggestion that the present laws discriminated against some traders. He said that some business people wanted totally deregulated trading hours or some change to the Sunday trading laws, but other traders thought that the present laws were the "best solution".

The Opposition spokesperson on small business, Mr Peter Loney, said that the Australian Labor Party did not favour total deregulation either. It would, he believed, disadvantage small retailers. He thought, however, that some exception to this would have to apply to certain tourist precincts in Melbourne.

(Adapted from an article by Victoria Gurvich, "Business Groups Call for Trading Hours Reshuffle", *Age*, 11 February 1995.)

... THE TOUGH GET GOING

BANK BASHERS

Australia's most profitable bank, National Australia Bank (NAB), hit back yesterday at bank bashers.

The managing director, Mr Don Argus, said the growing costs to the community of banking-related inquiries in recent years were "much larger" than many people realised. "I am very concerned at the unending series of inquiries that seem to be part and parcel of conducting banking operations in Australia," he told a meeting of business leaders.

He referred particularly to the Prices Surveillance Authority's recent inquiry into fees and charges by banks and other financial institutions. The PSA and some consumer groups seemed intent on establishing the banks' guilt before hearing any evidence, he said.

He said it seemed unfair that organisations like Telecom and Australia Post could get away with charging fees for customer services, while banks were being accused of a lack of social concern and responsibility.

Recent Reserve Bank of Australia and OECD reports, as well as those commissioned separately by the NAB itself, had shown that looking at countries with comparable banking systems, Australian banks had the lowest fees and charges and the second-highest interest rates on deposits.

Meanwhile, NAB - known for its aggressive competitiveness in the Australian banking industry - yesterday cut its fixed home loan rates for terms between two and five years by up to 1 per cent. NAB now has the cheapest fixed-interest rates of the four major banks and is much lower than the largest foreign bank in Australia, Citibank.

However, Mr Argus warned that unless the Federal Government was prepared to make substantial spending cuts in its forthcoming Budget, interest rates could rise to giddy levels over the next couple of years.

(Adapted from an article by Lisa Kearns, "NAB Criticises Bank Bashers", *Age*, 25 February 1995.)

Chapter 2: The Economist's View of Competition

CASE STUDY 2:

RUNNING OUT OF PUFF?

The Australian tobacco sector has all the hallmarks of a sunset industry. The market is shrinking, the potential for export growth is limited, production costs are among the highest in the world and, hamstrung by a virtual blanket ban on promoting the product, the major suppliers are locked in a three-way battle for market share.

Despite this, all three major tobacco companies continue to turn a profit.

Rothmans of Pall Mall (Australia) Ltd, the local subsidiary of British Tobacco giant Rothmans Plc., notched up a 51.2 per cent increase in net profit to $61 million last year. WD & HO Wills (Australia), 67 per cent owned by the UK-based BAT Industries announced profits of $50.7 million for the year to December 1993, and Philip Morris Ltd (Australia), a subsidiary of the giant multinational food and beverages group Philip Morris Companies Inc., makers of Marlboro cigarettes, Kraft Foods, Millers beer and Maxwell House coffee among others, turned in an impressive performance for the year ended 1993 with net profits of $46 million.

But it is not all beer and skittles for cigarette manufacturers.

The tobacco industry is one of the most highly regulated and highly taxed in Australia. The three local cigarette manufacturers forked out a hefty $1.39 billion in federal excise last year, and a further $1.9 billion in licence fees to the various state governments. It is anticipated that the industry will contribute more than $3.6 billion to the federal and state government coffers in 1994-95.

But not only do cigarette manufacturers have to contend with a tax system which imposes regular tax hikes on the product, none of which goes to the manufacturer. They also face a total ban on promoting the product. Manufacturers have been required to carry a health warning on cigarette packets since 1973, and radio and television advertisements for cigarette and tobacco products were banned in 1976.

Advertising in the print media was banned in 1990, and the Tobacco Prohibition Act, outlawing any written or audible message which promotes smoking, was introduced in 1992. From December 1995, cigarette companies will be banned from sponsoring sporting events, one of the few promotional opportunities remaining to them. Smoking has long been banned on public transport, and on domestic flights since 1987. A ban on smoking in commonwealth government offices followed in 1988, and this has now flowed through to most commercial offices.

So stringent are the bans that Philip Morris was forced to challenge the Tobacco Prohibition Act in the High Court last year when it was unable to place a product recall notice with any newspaper when it needed to recall a batch of faulty lighters.

Although the advertising and promotional bans have added an estimated $75 million a year to the companies' cash reserves, industry analysts believe that "without brand names the product is homogeneous, and the value of the brands is being whittled away without advertising support".

With their capacity to attract new smokers severely limited by the advertising bans, the cigarette companies are left slugging it out for as greater slice of the existing market.

The result is an intermittent price war.

Rothmans' Winfield brand dominated the Australian market for a decade before Wills launched the budget brand Horizon in the early 1990s in packs of fifty. The move prompted a price war which cost Rothmans dearly, slashing Winfield's market share from a shade over 22% in 1989 to about 16% in 1993. Over the same period, Horizon and Longbeach, the budget product quickly launched by Philip Morris, grabbed an impressive 25% of the total cigarette market.

Rothmans introduced Freedom early last year, sparking another round of discounting which cost the industry an estimated $8 million a week. Currently, the three cigarette makers are level-pegged, with local cigarette sales of around $950 million apiece, or around one-third of the market each.

With little prospect of increased sales at home, it would seem natural for the Australian manufacturers to look towards Asia, where the tobacco market is growing at an estimated 4 per cent a year.

So far, however, export sales are modest - and there are a number of reasons why this might continue to be the case.

To begin with, the tobacco excise and state fees make Australia's production costs high by world standards. Then, there is the matter of taste. Because the excise on tobacco leaf is so high, Australian manufacturers have developed a technique of "inflating" the leaf to reduce the amount of tobacco required in each cigarette. Although Australian smokers have clearly developed a taste for what are among the lightest cigarettes in the world, the change in flavour which results from the "inflating" is not popular overseas.

Finally, at least one of the Australian manufacturers is being squeezed out of potential overseas markets by its parent company; Wills is unlikely to take a serious interest in Asian markets because BAT is already heavily represented there.

Rothmans and Philip Morris, on the other hand, are at least keen to explore export opportunities, especially in PNG, Fiji, Vietnam and Malaysia. A Rothmans spokesperson has been quoted as saying that there is "significant growth potential" in Indonesia, "but it is extremely competitive, with strong local companies and strong overseas competitors". One Philip Morris executive believes that his company "has focused on exports over the last few years in a more serious manner than our competitors", but argues that the company's far-flung subsidiaries often have to compete against other Philip Morris divisions to win new export markets. "We have to show that we can produce a quality product at a competitive price", he said.

Chapter 2: The Economist's View of Competition

In the search for growth opportunities, there has also been much speculation about acquisitions by the cigarette manufacturers to broaden their market base. Foster's Brewing and the food group Goodman Fielder Wattie have recently been touted as possible Philip Morris acquisitions. However, a spokesperson for the company claims: "We have no present plans for any acquisitions of that nature in Australia. We are confident of a very solid future in the tobacco industry. We certainly don't see an acceleration in the rate of decline".

Similarly, a Wills spokesperson has claimed: "Wills is tobacco - we have no interest in buying anything else. Both we and our competitors are pretty aggressive, and our whole focus is to hold our market share and get business from our competitors".

In its attempt to remain competitive, Wills has slashed its workforce by several hundred and achieved hefty productivity gains. It has also achieved a significant improvement in quality, helped by a customer service program based on total quality management and "best practice" principles. It has stitched up a deal to share transport costs with its rival Philip Morris. It has upgraded its Pagewood (NSW) plant, purchasing new high-speed equipment which will further improve productivity and quality.

Rothmans, too, has worked hard to streamline its operations and improve efficiency. It is aware that its market share has slipped from 41 per cent five years ago to its present level of a third, and it is keen to recover the lost ground.

So far, the biggest threat to the tobacco industry has failed to materialise - legal action by smokers claiming addiction, suffering and pain. Unlike the U.S., where court action has centred on claims that the cigarette companies deliberately hid the fact that smoking is addictive, smoking-related litigation in Australia to date has been limited to passive smoking cases directed against various employers for failing to provide a safe environment. While several cases have been brought by smokers claiming compensation for damage to their health, so far none have stuck.

Nor is it likely that governments will ever wish to legislate tobacco manufacturers out of existence - they have 3.6 billion good reasons a year not to kill off the industry altogether!

(Adapted from an article by Margaret Lyons, "Not Running Out of Puff", *ABM*, April 1995, pp. 54-58.)

Competitive Advantage: Concepts and Cases

CASE STUDY - QUESTIONS FOR DISCUSSION

1. Philip Morris is one of the major players in the tobacco industry? Who are its competitors? (Be careful!)

2. What specific characteristics of the Australian tobacco industry make the going so tough? Explain.

3. If rivalry between the major players in the industry is as fierce as the case suggest, why would W.D. & H.O. Wills be pleased to have "stitched up a deal" with a competitor to share transport costs?

4. Why would Philip Morris want its "far-flung" divisions to compete with each other for export markets?

5. What is meant by the phrase "without brand names, the product is homogeneous"? How does advertising support brand building and product differentiation?

6. According to the case, $75 million dollars of expense was saved each year by the three companies when the Government banned cigarette advertising and promotion. If so, shouldn't the companies be pleased?

7. What does the term "productivity" really mean? Wouldn't the fact that Wills has "slashed" its workforce *reduce* (rather than *increase*) productivity?

8. "Taste" appears to be one serious barrier to export sales of Australian cigarettes. What do you think could be done, both here and abroad, to overcome the problem?

9. Can you justify the Government's desire, from an ethical point of view, of wanting to keep the tobacco industry alive while it regulates and taxes it so heavily?

10. What are the "best practice" principles? What, precisely, would the implementation of these principles involve?

11. Wills has adopted a "total quality management" approach to its customer service program. What does this imply? Who would Wills consider to be its customers?

Competitive Advantage and the Marketing Discipline

As we have seen in the previous chapter, much of what we understand about the nature of competition has come to us from the discipline of economics. Traditionally, economists have classified competition within industries, largely on the basis of the number of sellers involved, into market types of pure competition, monopolistic competition, oligopolistic competition and pure monopoly.

Using these basic structures, economists have been able to isolate, define and predict many facets of competitive behaviour.

The economist's view of competition, however, has not always been of immediate help to business managers faced with the demands of survival and growth in dynamic and hostile environments. Consciously or unconsciously, they have turned elsewhere in their search for better ways to compete and for better guides to competitive strategy formulation.

In Search of Competitive Advantage: Alternative Managerial Orientations or "Mind-Sets"

In searching for a competitive advantage, a number of different business management orientations (or philosophies, concepts or "mind-sets") have emerged - the *production philosophy*, the *product philosophy*, the *selling philosophy*, the *marketing philosophy* and the *societal marketing philosophy*.

Each of these different philosophies has had, and still retains, its adherents.

Since the 1950s, however, in a market-place that has become considerably tougher as the ability to supply as outstripped customer demand, as deregulation and technology have proliferated choices, many enterprises have turned to the *marketing philosophy* to provide a profitable business base. Today, in fact, in most successful businesses, the adoption of the marketing philosophy is seen to have been a critical component of their rise to prominence.

More recently, in the wake of the unprecedented interest of consumers in environmental issues, business managers have increasingly turned their attention to the *societal marketing philosophy* which, because it relies on the same fundamental principles as the marketing philosophy can be seen as an enhancement of it rather than as a distinctly new philosophy.

As both the marketing philosophy and the societal marketing philosophy can be seen to have evolved from the philosophies which preceded them (production philosophy, product philosophy, selling philosophy) we must briefly examine each of them before considering the marketing philosophy.

Production Concept

Production-oriented managers see *internal efficiency* and *cost control* the prime competitive weapons.

Managers with a production "mind-set" believe that customers will consistently favour producers whose goods and services are cheaper, and in plentiful supply.

They assume that the key to the achievement of organisational goals lies in increasing production volume to achieve unit cost reduction, and price advantage if necessary. They assume that there will be a continuing high level of demand.

The production philosophy is characterised by an internal focus and a disregard of customer preferences. Henry Ford, often cited as a manager typifying those with a production "mind-set" is reported to have said: "My customers can have their cars in any colour they want - as long as it's black!"

The attitudes to their customers of the management and staff of some big government instrumentalities, such as those responsible for the telecommunications, social security, railways, motor registrations, water, gas and electricity, and so on, have often been used to exemplify the production "mind-set". They know that their customers have no choice but to buy the goods and services they offer from them - because what they provide are essential services, and their organisations are the sole providers of them. They have often been accused of treating their customers with a "take-it-or-leave-it" attitude.

From the point of view of the management and staff of such organisations, however, attitudes such as these have often made good sense. Their objective has been to have their goods and services readily available, at the lowest possible cost, to large numbers of customers. Focusing on their own efficiency, standardising their offerings, and treating all customers in much the same way, has been seen as the most effective way to carry out their obligations.

It is fair to say, however, that as governments deregulate and privatise industries and open them up to competition, senior management is quickly coming to an understanding that the production mentality or "mind-set" is no longer adequate. When customers have a choice of suppliers, they will obviously deal with the firm whose offer, in all its dimensions, best suits their needs and wants.

Today, in fact, the production "mind-set" is probably best typified by those in smaller, privately-owned business enterprises (such as some medical, legal and other professional services practices) were management and staff see a continuing high demand for the goods and services they offer, and where there are relatively few providers of realistic substitutes.

Now, there is nothing at all wrong with an organisation having a concern for internal efficiency and keeping a close watch on its costs. Marketplace success will often depend on those elements of the business. But, to focus on those aspects in expectation that they alone can provide a competitive edge is dangerous. A high volume of production, at low cost, in the most efficient manner possible, are useless if the organisation's product does not find market acceptance.

Chapter 3: Competitive Advantage and the Marketing Discipline

Product Concept

Product-oriented managers see *product quality* as the prime competitive weapon.

Managers with a product "mind-set" believe that customers will consistently favour the producer whose goods and services are of a superior quality.

They assume that the key to the achievement of organisational goals lies in increasing product quality to a level beyond that of other competitors. Thus, it, too, has an internal focus. And, like the earlier production philosophy, it assumes a high continuity of demand.

But do customers always favour the producer whose quality is the highest? The answer, of course, is that they do not.

Does McDonald's sell the best quality food? Does IBM make the best quality computers? Do all car owners buy Pirelli tyres?

Often, higher quality means higher price, and for this reason many customers will choose to buy a product that is cheaper. Sometimes, to obtain the product which is of superior quality will necessitate a delay or some other inconvenience, such as having to travel a long distance to the shop which sells it. Many customers will prefer not to have to wait, or to put themselves to inconvenience. They will settle for a product of less quality.

Moreover, it is not always possible for customers to know which product, of several that might be available, is the one which is of superior quality. Would you, for example, know which make of VCR on the market is of the best quality? Say that you assume that the highest-priced machine is of better quality than its competitors. Is your assumption necessarily correct?

For reasons such as these, the product philosophy has sometimes been referred to as "the mouse-trap fallacy". Ralph Waldo Emerson, the American philosopher and writer, once said: "If a man can preach a better sermon, write a better book, or build a better mouse-trap, even though he hide it in his house deep in the woods, the world will beat a path to his door." But, as many an impoverished inventor of a better mouse-trap can testify, this just isn't the case!

Of course, there is nothing at all wrong with an organisation having a good product. Often, marketplace success will depend on it. And there is nothing at all wrong with having the best product; all manufacturers would like to be in that position.

But, to focus on product quality as a sure-fire means to a competitive edge - without regard to the other dimensions on which customers make their purchase decisions - is a dangerous course of action.

Selling Concept

Selling-oriented managers see *promotion* - forceful advertising and the persistent hard-sell - as the prime competitive weapon.

Managers with a selling "mind-set" believe that customers will consistently favour the producer whose goods and services are most widely and vigorously promoted.

Competitive Advantage: Concepts and Cases

They assume that the key to the achievement of organisational goals lies in the communication of the virtues of the product to existing and potential customer groups more aggressively than competitors. Thus, it, too, has an internal focus. And, as with the earlier production and philosophies, they assume a high continuity of demand and increasing supply.

This is not to say that having a strong and persistent sales force is not a good thing, or that expenditure on advertising is wasteful. Often, marketplace success depends on their use in the business mix.

But to focus on them as the sole, or even the prime, means to a competitive advantage is not wise. Both, to some extent, may confer a short-term advantage; they may convince customers to try the product once. But if the customers (unless there is a never-ending number of them), having tried the product once, do not return to buy again and again, the business must eventually decline and fail.

Marketing Concept

Marketing-oriented managers see *the satisfaction of customer needs and wants* as the prime competitive weapon.

It assumes that the key to the achievement of organisational goals lies in the accurate identification of the needs and wants of target customers and in the delivery of the desired satisfactions more efficiently and effectively than competitors.

Managers with a marketing "mind-set" believe that customers will consistently favour the producer whose goods and services most precisely match their needs and wants. They understand, however, that the needs and wants of customers in any market are likely to differ markedly.

They make, therefore, a very careful study of the market (market research), to identify the various kinds of needs and wants that exist (market segmentation), to select those groups of customers whose needs they believe they can satisfy better than competitors (targeting), and to arrange for their offerings to these groups to be perceived as different to, and more valuable than, those of competitors (positioning).

Thus, marketing has an external focus. It does not assume a high continuity of demand. In fact, in direct contrast to the three philosophies already discussed, it assumes that supply will out-strip demand.

Marketing's catch-cries are "Love the Customer, not the Product", "The Customer is King (or Queen)", and "Customer Sovereignty".

The marketing-oriented manager asks, "Who are our customers? What are their needs and wants? What can we make that they will buy? How can we price, promote and distribute our goods and services in a way that best suits our customers." The marketing-oriented manager is, of course, concerned with internal efficiency, product quality, and promotion, but these are less central considerations. At the centre of his or her philosophy is the thought that unless the customer is satisfied with the offering - in all its dimensions - that customer will turn to a competitor's offering and the firm's objectives will not be met.

Chapter 3: Competitive Advantage and the Marketing Discipline

Explaining marketing-oriented thinking, Peter Drucker, the U.K. management academic has said: "The aim of marketing is to make selling unnecessary".[1] Selling will never be unnecessary, but it is not difficult to understand what Drucker meant: If a firm can produce a product that precisely satisfies the needs and wants of its targeted customers, what need will there be to "sell" it to them?

A very similar thought has been expressed by the U.S. academic, Theodore Levitt: "Selling is getting rid of what you have; marketing is having what you can get rid of."[2] What Levitt implies is that "selling" your product is a short-term approach to customers; you may well be able "to get rid of what you have", but will you be able to entice your customers to buy again. Marketing, on the other hand, is a long-term approach; if you have "what you can get rid of", customers will certainly return for more.

Today, firms which subscribe to the marketing philosophy concentrate their endeavours on marshaling and directing their resources to the satisfaction of the needs and wants of existing and potential customers. They do this, not because they are intrinsically noble or generous or good-willed, but because they see this as the surest means by which they can attract - and retain - an adequate customer base.

Effective marketing calls for organising and planning (having the right people and the right company structure); identifying market opportunities (understanding the environment, conducting marketing research, understanding the buying behaviour of customers); selecting target markets (segmenting the market, targeting and positioning); developing a marketing mix for the targeted customers (blending product, price, promotion, place into a synergistic whole offering); and implementing, controlling and evaluating marketing programs (delivering the marketing "promise").

Societal Marketing Concept

Societal-marketing oriented managers see *the satisfaction of customer needs and wants* and *a concern with social responsibility* as the prime competitive weapons.

Societal-marketing oriented managers believe that customers will respond more favourably to those firms which show that they are societally responsible, responsive to society's best interests and good corporate citizens.

Emerging in the early seventies in the wake of the Oil Crisis and the subsequent heightened consciousness of the finite nature of the earth's resources, the societal marketing concept should be seen not so much as an alternative business philosophy, but as an enhancement of the prevailing marketing philosophy.

In recognising the growing consumer concern with the environment and with the well-being of society, many marketers have focused their attention on the satisfaction of customer needs and wants while maintaining the best interests of society. In this, they recognise that environmental protection and social responsibility of all kinds are paramount in the needs and wants of customers.

Today, the marketing philosophy (with its enhanced societal emphasis) is subscribed to by most of the world's leading business organisations. They consider it crucial to their on-going success.

It, they believe, can best provide their firms with a competitive edge.

Marketing is Competitive Advantage

Speaking at a marketing conference in Melbourne recently, a prominent academic startled his audience when he suggested, very seriously, that the time had come to make a change to the name of the marketing discipline. When asked by a conference delegate to propose a new name, he replied: "Competitive Advantage".

He went on to explain that, in a sense, every managerial orientation is adopted (consciously or unconsciously) because management believes that that orientation will most readily allow the organisation to be a "winner" in its industry.

In today's business climate, when in nearly every market sector there is an excess of supply over demand, the adoption of the marketing concept - the assumption that the surest way to achieve the goals and objectives of the organisation is identify the needs and wants of targeted groups of customers and to deliver their satisfactions more effectively than rivals can - **is** a competitive advantage.

Marketing and Competitive Strategy

With its own collection of concepts, tools and techniques of analysis, the marketing discipline has provided its adherents with a number of new insights into competitive strategy.

In the remainder of this chapter we will devote our attention to four of them:

- marketing's new classification of competitors
- competitor analysis from the marketing perspective
- the concept of market position
- the product life cycle concept

In these four marketing concerns are issues of significance to our quest for competitive advantage.

A New Classification of Competitors

When marketing theory began to surface as the discipline emerged as the dominant business philosophy in the 1950s and 1960s, academics and practitioners alike soon found it necessary to reject the economist's classification of competitors. While they acknowledged that it had served economists well for many decades, it was too narrow and restrictive, and too limited in its applications, for their own purposes.

"Is it really so", they asked, "that a wheat farmer is in competition only with other wheat farmers, as economic theory implies?"

"Is it really a fact that a manufacturer of soap (or toothpaste) is in competition only with other manufacturers of soap (or toothpaste)?"

Chapter 3: Competitive Advantage and the Marketing Discipline

"Is it really true that a monopolist has no competition at all?" For instance, if we own the only movie theatre in a small, remote country town, the economist would say that we are in a monopoly situation (as we have seen in our previous chapter.) But, does this mean that we have no competition at all?

From the marketer's perspective, it seems clear that we may well have a great deal of competition. That competition might come from the local bowling alley, the ice-skating rink, the race-track, the pin-ball parlour, the hamburger shop, or numerous other sources of a similar kind.

Considerations such as these have led marketing theorists to an alternative view of competitive situations: *desire competitors, generic competitors, product-form competitors,* and *brand competitors.*

Let us now see what each of these categories imply.

Desire Competitors

These are businesses which are in competition for the whole range of goods and services which we, as consumers, may desire, or wish to purchase, with our discretionary income.

Assume that a young couple have saved hard and have $5,000 in their bank account. They sit down to decide what they would like to spend it on. One suggests that it would good to take a holiday; the other thinks that it would be wiser to upgrade the car or to make some home improvements.

In this sense, holiday destinations (and the airlines or travel agents which service them) are in competition with car manufacturers and also with firms which renovate houses. All are competing for the custom of our young couple.

Generic Competitors

These are businesses which provide the same broad category of good or service, yet whose offerings may be quite dissimilar in kind.

Assume, for instance, that our young couple decides to renovate their home. Home renovations can take many forms. The couple may decide to put in a new kitchen. They may decide to have a new front fence built. They may decide to give their home a new coat of paint.

All of the providers of renovation services such as these are generic competitors. Thus, kitchen manufacturers compete with fence builders. Both compete with paint manufacturers.

Product-Form Competitors

These are businesses which provide the same kind of good or service but in a different form.

Assume, for instance, that our young couple decides to have a new front fence built. They may decide to have it built from bricks. They may decide to have a timber-picket fence built. They may decide to have it built using volcanic rock or stone.

All of the suppliers of these materials (similar in kind but different in form) are in this sense in competition with each other.

Brand Competitors

These are businesses which offer different brands of an equivalent good or service.

Thus, if our young couple decides to build a brick fence, they might decide to buy "Clifton" bricks, or "Nu-Brick" bricks, or "Victor" bricks, or any other brand of brick.

Obviously, all competitors in a market selling brands of a product for the same use or purpose are in competition with each other.

Competitor Analysis

In Chapter 1, the point was made that in today's hostile and dynamic environment, an understanding of a firm's competitors is just as important for success as an understanding of its customers.

To determine their customers' needs and wants - so that the desired satisfactions can be delivered to them more efficiently and effectively than competitors are able to - marketers need to have the answers to questions such as these: Who are our customers? Why do they buy? How do they buy? Who makes the buying decision? What do they buy? When do they buy? Where do they buy?

In the same way, to understand their competitors - so that they can develop and implement more effective marketing plans and programs than their competitors - marketers need to have the answers to questions such as: Who are our competitors? What are their objectives? What are their strategies? What are their assumptions? What are their strengths and weaknesses? What is our competitive advantage? What is their competitive advantage? What are their likely reactions to their rivals' initiatives? Which competitors ought to be attacked, and which ought to be avoided? How can competitive information of this kind be gathered?

A guide to the provision of answers to the first set of questions here (those relating to the understanding of customers) is beyond the scope of this book. We must now, however, turn our attention to the second set of questions: those which relate to an understanding of competitors.

Who are our Competitors?

In the preceding section of this chapter, we have examined the broad way in which those who subscribe to the marketing philosophy approach this question.

There, however, our discussion was largely confined to an "industry" view of competitors. Our aim was to highlight the differences in the approach to competitor definition between marketers and economists.

But marketers need to take a "market" view of competition as well.

Chapter 3: Competitive Advantage and the Marketing Discipline

To illustrate, on the *industry* level, the Coca-Cola Company might define its competitors (for its mainstream "Coke" product) as the Water Board; the dairy industry; tea, coffee and cocoa producers; beer and spirit manufacturers; fruit juice manufacturers, and so on. But, on a *market* level, it will define its competitors differently. Pepsico is one formidable rival; Cadbury Schweppes is another; the Coles Myer group (which sells its "AC Cola" brand through its K Mart outlets) is yet another. These are *direct* competitors to the Coca-Cola Company in the Australian soft-drink market.

What are our Competitors' Objectives?

To answer to this question depends on the marketer being able to discover what each competitor is doing in the market and what motivates its behaviour.

A competitor's objectives may be shaped by its size and history, by the motivations of its current managers, by whether it is an independent firm or part of a larger corporation, and so on.

Depending on factors such as these, the objectives of firms in a market can vary significantly. Some are in the market, primarily, to maximise profits; others have the prime objective of generating cash flow, others of developing technology to be used in more important markets. There can be many other objectives, too. And some firms have mixed objectives rather than a single objective.

Some firms want quick profits, others are prepared to wait; some firms have global expansion goals, others do not.

The point is, of course, that marketers need to understand the goals of all significant rivals - and those of all rivals which may become significant at some time in the foreseeable future.

How may the goals and objectives of competitors be assessed? There is no quick answer. Some marketers have devised tools and techniques (the market battlefield grid, for instance) to assist them in the task.³ For most marketers, however, it is a matter of constant monitoring and careful gathering of competitive data over time.

What are our Competitors' Strategies?

Many marketers attempt to answer this question by mapping the competitors in a market by "strategic group".

A strategic group is a group of competitors in a market who appear to follow the same broad strategies to achieve their ends. These strategies may include, for example, their approach to product quality, or pricing, or promotion, or distribution channels. They might also include their approach to manufacturing, R&D and human resource management. They might also include their approach to vertical integration.

Within any market there is likely to be a number of strategic groups of competitors. While rivalry is likely to be at its most intense between competitors in the same strategic group, it may also be intense between the groups themselves.

Competitive Advantage: Concepts and Cases

Understanding the strategic groupings in a market can help a competitor to formulate strategies for success. For example, when Coles Myer's K Mart decided to launch its "AC Cola" product a year or two ago, it must surely have been aware that the strategic group it would have to contend with included the giants, Coca-Cola and Pepsico. Because of its financial strength and distribution channel power, K Mart was obviously not daunted by the task. But if it *had* seen this task as too being difficult, it may have chosen to compete against less formidable rivals in some other strategic grouping, perhaps with those in the "non-cola" segment of the market.

What are our Competitors' Assumptions?

Every competitor in the market works on certain assumptions. If we can determine our competitors' assumptions correctly, we can gain a distinct competitive advantage over them.

Suppose that one of the industry rivals *assumes* that a large sales force is a key ingredient for success in a particular market. The cost to that rival of maintaining its large sales force will be high. If the assumption is incorrect, any competitor which can communicate effectively to its customer groups without at lower cost will obtain a considerable cost advantage over it.

Or, suppose that one of the industry rivals *assumes* that frequent new product introductions, or high inventory level, or high service level, or a large branch network, or any other expensive-to-maintain aspect of operations, is a key requirement for success. Competitors who understand that their rival's assumptions are incorrect stand to gain a significant competitive advantage.

The question of how the incorrect assumptions of industry rivals are ascertained is, again, not easy to answer. As discussed above, constant monitoring and careful gathering of competitive data is the logical starting point.

What are our Competitors' Strengths and Weaknesses?

Every one of our competitors in the market has its strengths and weaknesses, and these should be understood if an advantage over them is to be developed.

These strengths and weaknesses relate to a competitor's resources and capabilities. They include, of course, such variables as annual sales volume, current market share, return on investment, cash flow, new investment allocation, and capacity utilisation.

These, and other strength and weakness variables such as product quality, product availability and technical service capabilities, often become available through personal contact with the representatives of rival firms, through membership of trade associations, through the "hearsay" of suppliers and customers, and through the trade press and other published sources.

In addition, wise marketing managers will continually monitor the customer awareness and brand loyalty levels of all competitors (including, certainly, those of their own company).

What is our Competitive Advantage? What is their Competitive Advantage?

All firms have certain values as perceived by customers. Some may offer their product at lower prices; some may provide better a back-up service; some may offer the advantage of a more convenient location, and so on. These values are those firms' competitive advantage.

Chapter 3: Competitive Advantage and the Marketing Discipline

Marketers often group their customers by value orientation, dividing the market into segments according to what each segment perceives to be most valuable. In this way, they can avoid segments in which strong competitors offer value which they cannot match.

What are our Competitors' Reaction Patterns?

Knowing each competitor's likely reaction pattern to given circumstances can help marketers to plan appropriately.

Some competitors in a market always react savagely to competitive initiatives (such as price reductions, new product introductions, and new entrants to the market); others are always more passive.

Some will react strongly at times, but ignore competitors' moves at other times; others will react strongly to the moves of particular competitors, but not to those of other competitors.

Armed with the knowledge of a competitor's typical reaction pattern, marketers can gain significant competitive advantages by luring it to react. For instance, if a firm cuts its price by 10% knowing that its competitor will react with a price reduction of 15%, it might gain a significant advantage when the market demand is elastic.

Which Competitors should we Attack? Which should we Avoid?

Many firms concentrate on attacking smaller and weaker competitors, knowing that taking market share from them requires less effort and fewer resources. The problem with this, however, is that the smaller and weaker firms often have less to teach their competitors about how to succeed. Larger and stronger firms usually have weaknesses too, and in attacking them, a competitor can improve its capabilities in the market.

Harvard's Michael E. Porter has made a distinction between "good" and "bad" competitors, advising companies to support the "good" competitors in their markets and to attack the "bad". By "good" competitors, he means those which understand the market, care about it, and want it to grow. By "bad", he means those which do not play by the rules. They are destructive in their approach, setting prices which undermine the ability of caring firms to produce adequate profit margins, or offering poor or minimal service. They appear to be in the market only for short-term, opportunistic reasons, and have little real interest in its long-term viability.[4]

How can Competitive Intelligence be Gathered?

To answer these questions firms need to gather competitive data. Some companies have formal approaches to the collection of data, others use informal approaches.

Taking a formal approach, some firms invest in complex marketing information systems - a dedicated group of people using computer technology to gather, sort, analyse, evaluate data, and to disseminate accurate and timely information to managers to assist their decision-making. This information includes that which is gathered about competitors.[5]

Company recruits and the employees of competitors are informal sources of competitive data. Often, in interviewing applicants for advertised positions, a company will speak to a competitor's present and former employees.

Customers, suppliers, consultants and other intermediaries who come in contact with competitors are another such source of competitive data.

Published materials and public documents provide much competitive data.

Sometimes, companies will seek out and purchase the products of competitors. Analysis of this physical evidence, or "reverse engineering", can provide much data about costs, quality, manufacturing processes and so on.

The Concept of Market Position

Another significant contribution to the theory of competitive advantage from the marketing discipline is the concept of *market position*.

In any market, competitors will differ in their resources and capabilities, objectives and assumptions. Some firms will be large, some will be small, some will be somewhere in between.

Because of this, they will occupy different positions in the market. Some will strive to be market leaders, others will have to be followers. Thus, their competitive strategies will be determined by their market position.

These different positions have been categorised in a number of ways.

The Arthur D. Little Classification

The management consulting firm, Arthur D. Little, has classified organisations using the following six different positions in the industry.

Dominant: the firm controls the behaviour of other competitors and has a wide choice of strategic options.

Strong: the firm can take independent action without endangering its long-term position and can maintain its long-term position regardless of competitors' actions.

Favourable: the firm has a strength that is exploitable in particular strategies and has more than average opportunity to improve its position.

Tenable: the firm is performing at a sufficiently satisfactory level to warrant continuing in business, but it exists at the sufferance of the dominant company and has a less than average opportunity to improve its position.

Weak: the firm has unsatisfactory performance but an opportunity exists for improvement and it must change or else exit.

Non-viable: the firm has unsatisfactory performance and no opportunity for improvement.

The Ries and Trout Classification

In their book, *Marketing Warfare* (McGraw Hill, New York, 1986), the prominent marketing consultants Al Ries and Jack Trout have provided another example of market position categorisation.

They see firms as occupying any of four different positions in a market:

Defensive: the firm is the dominant force in the market; its strategy must be aimed at holding its market share, and defending its position.

Offensive: the firm is the "second player" in the market; its strategy must be aimed at increasing its market share by taking share from the dominant player and/or smaller players.

Flanking: the firm is a smaller player; it strategy must be aimed at increasing its market share by attacking the flanks (points of weaknesses) of its rivals; it should avoid head to-head battles with the stronger players.

Guerilla: the firm is a minor player; it can, however, be successful if it looks for small (or specialised) segments of the market which the larger players overlook or avoid.

A More Standard Classification

Yet another classification of market position (and perhaps the most common one) is that which is offered by Philip Kotler and a number of other writers in the marketing discipline.[6]

They, too, describe four market positions, referring to them as:

Market Leader: the firm which has the largest share in the relevant product market.

Market Challenger: a firm which has a relatively large share of the market, but a smaller share than the market leader.

Market Follower: a firm which holds a market share smaller than the market leader or potential challenger; it prefers to follow rather than to attack.

Market Nicher: a smaller firm which targets segments within segments (or market niches).

Each of these market positions provides the occupant with the opportunity to be a "winner" - provided, of course, that the occupant recognises its true position in the market and formulates strategies that are appropriate to that position.

That is, to be a winner, a market leader must employ market leader strategies, a market challenger *must* employ market challenger strategies, and so on. If a leader acts like a challenger, it will be a loser; if a challenger acts like a follower, it will be a loser; if a nicher tries to act like a leader, it will be a loser, and so on.

What, then, are the appropriate strategies for each market position?

Strategies for the Market Leader

The market leader has three prime strategies:

- *defending* its position in the market, it must hold its market dominance.

- *attacking* smaller players, it must improve its market share.

- *expanding the total market*, it must increase overall demand for its products.

Kodak in photography, Xerox in copying, Coca-Cola in soft-drinks and McDonalds in fast-foods are examples of dominant market leaders.

There are a number of ways in which a company can *defend* its position in the market:

- position defense: the company continues to do what it is already doing but does it better.

- flanking defense: the company identifies its points of weakness and guards against attacks upon them by competitors.

- pre-emptive defense: the company launches an attack on a competitor before the competitor attacks it.

- counter-defensive defense: the company strikes back aggressively against any competitor's attack.

- mobile defense: the company increases it strength by entering new geographic territories and/or new market segments, and by diversifying into other businesses.

- contraction defense: the company recognises that it has a weakness which it cannot properly defend and deliberately chooses to move out of that product-market, using its resources in a more beneficial way.

These defense strategies are illustrated in Figure 3.1.

Chapter 3: Competitive Advantage and the Marketing Discipline

Fig. 3.1: Defence Strategies

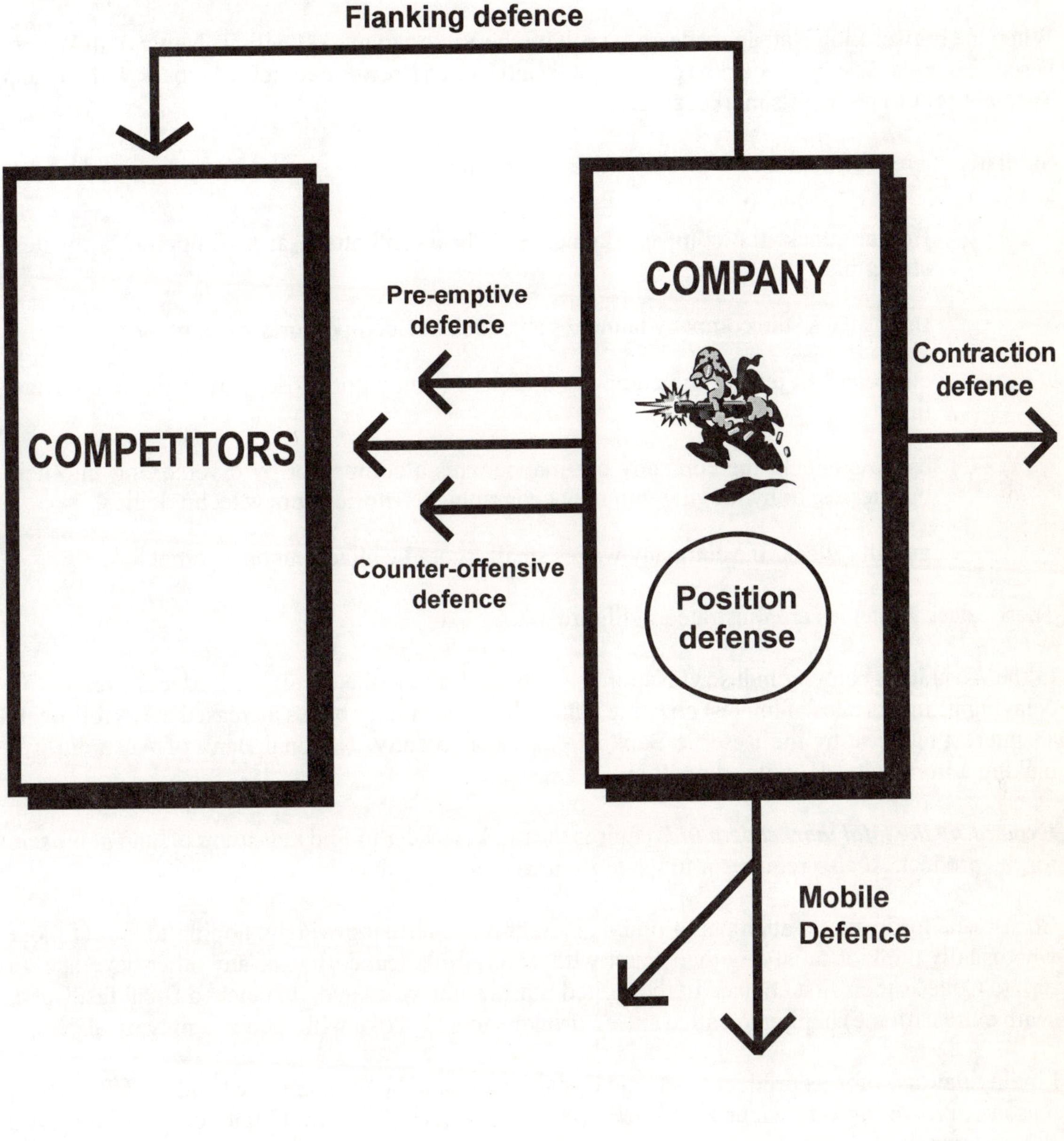

Source: Kotler, P., Chandler, P.C., Brown, L. and Adam, S., *Marketing in Australia and New Zealand*, Prentice Hall of Australia, Sydney, 3rd edition, 1994, p. 659.

Competitive Advantage: Concepts and Cases

In recent times, we have seen many good examples of strong market leaders protecting their positions using some or other of these defensive tactics. For instance, when the giant U.S. retailer Toys "R" Us announced its plans to open stores in Australia, Coles Myer moved swiftly to protect the dominant position it had in the toy market in Australia (through its K Mart outlets) by setting up a new division, World For Kids.

When the brewer Lion Nathan made an assault on the Victorian market with its New South Wales-based Toohey's Blue light beer, the giant Carlton and United Breweries quickly hit back with Fosters Special Light to protect its market share.

Similarly, there are a number of ways in which a company can *attack* smaller players to build market share:

- frontal attack: the company launches a "head-on" attack at a competitor's greatest strength.

- flank attack: the company launches an attack at a competitor's weak point.

- encirclement attack: the company attacks a competitor on several fronts at the same time.

- by-pass attack: the company out-manoeuvres a competitor by diversifying into new businesses, or by moving into new geographic territories or new technologies.

- guerilla attack: the company wages small, sporadic attacks upon a competitor.

These attack strategies are illustrated in Figure 3.2.

In the Australian banking industry, National Australia Bank is the dominant leader at present. In delaying lifting its rates of interest on home loans when other major banks increased theirs following an interest rate rise by the Reserve Bank of Australia recently, National Bank of Australia was making a frontal attack on its competitors.

Expanding the total market demand requires the market leader to find *new users* of, and *new users* for, its product. It also requires it to get *more usage* of its product.

Coca-Cola, for instance, attempts to find *new users* by advertising widely, hoping to attract those who usually think of satisfying their thirst with water, milk, tea, coffee, or any other beverage, to turn to Coke as their first choice. In the United States some years ago, it launched Breakfast Coke, (with extra caffeine) hoping to entice coffee-drinkers to take Coke with their morning meal.

Finding *new uses* for its product is a tactic Coca-Cola would be unlikely to consider - for obvious reasons. Promoting it as a laundry bleach or as an insect repellant would not be wise. However, some companies have used such tactics successfully. The well-recorded example is that of Arm and Hammer Baking Powder. When sales of baking powder, a cooking ingredient, began to decline some years ago, the market leader, Arm and Hammer, found new uses for its product, promoting it as a deodoriser for use in refrigerators and on carpets.

Coca-Cola attempts to encourage *more usage* of its product in a number of ways, the most obvious of which is its use of larger bottles.

Fig. 3.2: Attack Strategies

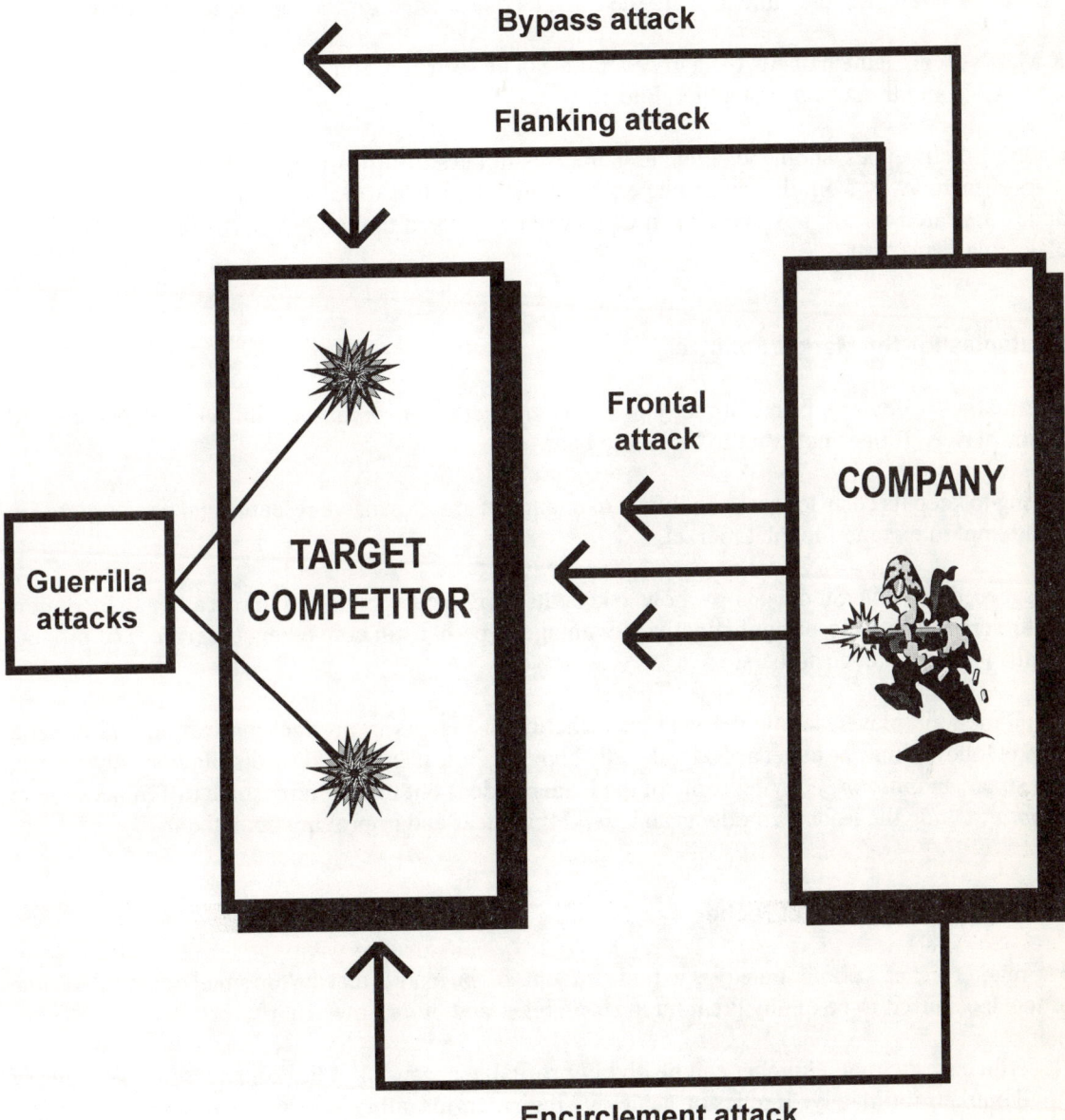

Source: Kotler, P., Chandler, P.C., Brown, L. and Adam, S., *Marketing in Australia and New Zealand*, Prentice Hall of Australia, Sydney, 3rd edition, 1994, p. 661.

Strategies for the Market Challenger

The market challenger's prime strategy is to *attack* other players. It can attempt to wrest market share from the market leader, or from the smaller players, or from both.

The attack strategies available to it are the same as those listed for the market leader, above.

K Mart's recent launch of AC Cola in Australia can be seen as a frontal attack on the market leader, Coca-Cola and the strong challenger, Pepsi.

Cadbury-Schweppes, another challenger in the Australian soft-drink industry, recently tried to wrest market share away from the larger players by launching Clear Cola, a colourless cola drink. The attack appeared to fail, however, when Coca-Cola countered the move with its launch of its own clear cola, Tab Clear.

Strategies for the Market Follower

The market follower's prime strategy is to *avoid direct confrontation* with the better-resourced major player. It does not want to "rock the boat".

Trying to keep its costs low, it is not likely to engage in any expensive research and development in an attempt to expand the total market.

To succeed, however, it must know how to keep its current customers and to win a fair share of new customers as it tries to bring distinctive advantages, (perhaps in convenience, services or product quality) to its target customers.

As a "me-too" player, taking the lead from the major players in product innovation and price, a market follower may be either a *cloner,* directly copying the leader's products, distribution, advertising, and so on; an *imitator,* copying some of the leader's ideas but maintaining some differences; or an *adaptor,* taking the leader's products and marketing ideas and improving upon them.

Strategies for the Market Nicher

The market nicher's prime strategy is to find segments of the market that are too small, too troublesome or too specialised to be of any great interest to bigger and more powerful players.

Nevertheless, the market nicher can be highly profitable because it relies on knowing the needs of small markets intimately. It relies on achieving high margins rather than high volumes.

There are many kinds of market nichers. Some concentrate on particular geographic areas, some on servicing particular industries, some on producing particular products or parts, and so on.

The dangers of a niching strategy are that the niche might dry up, or, if very successful, might attract the attention of a major player. For this reason, *multiple niching is* often preferred to *single niching.*

Chapter 3: Competitive Advantage and the Marketing Discipline

Insights into Competitive Strategy and Competitive Advantage from Product Life Cycle Theory

Marketing theorists and practitioners have long valued the product life cycle (PLC) concept for the insights it can provide into competitive strategy.

Acknowledging its many shortcomings, they understand that its value lies, not in the rigid application of its prescriptives, but in the implication that each stage of the life cycle warrants different marketing objectives, strategies and tactical programs.

Each stage of the life cycle represents a different marketing challenge.

At the *introductory* stage, the challenge is to build category awareness (or primary demand) by achieving the acceptance of innovators and influencers.

In *growth*, as competitors enter the market, it is to establish market position by ensuring consistency of quality and supply, and by building customer preference for the company's brand (or selective demand).

During *maturity*, it is to maintain and improve profitability by defending market position (perhaps by product enhancements) while searching for new growth segments.

In *decline*, it is to sustain profitability by cost reduction and price manipulation while planning for market exit at the appropriate time.

These four fundamental stages of the product life cycle are well understood. However, a number of marketing theorists have found it useful to propose another stage in the product life cycle - the *competitive turbulence* stage. This stage occurs between growth and maturity, and is illustrated in Figure 3.3.

Fig. 3.3: Life Cycle of a Typical Product Showing the Competitive Turbulence Stage

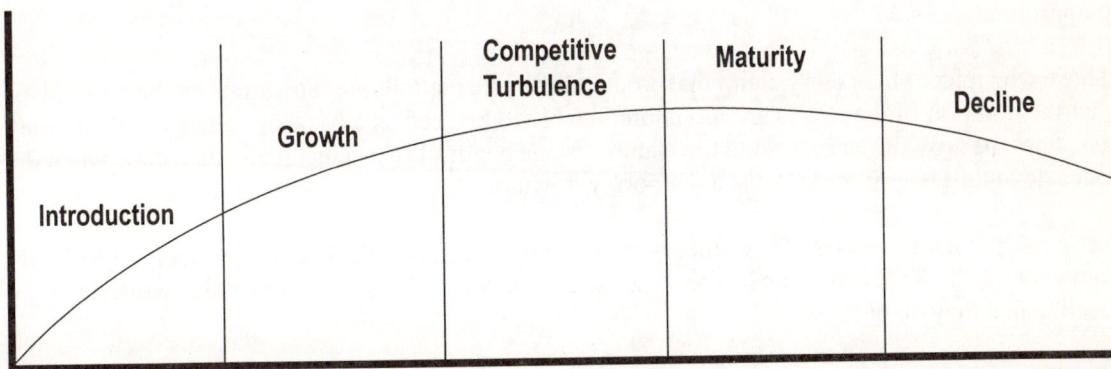

Competitive Turbulence Stage Strategies

Recognition of the competitive turbulence stage enhances the contribution which product life cycle theory can make to an analysis of the changing patterns of competition and to the formulation of competitive strategy. The challenges which present themselves at this stage are decidedly more difficult to deal with than at any other stage.[7]

At this stage, the entry of new competitors and the increase in capacity by entrenched players leads to an over-supply of product at a time when demand is slackening as market saturation approaches or as technology alternatives become available. Because it is a stage of heightened competitive activity, often marked by price cutting, declining profitability and a consequent struggle for survival, it is sometimes referred to as the "shakeout" stage.

Figure 3.4 shows the marketing strategies by which a company attempts to compete successfully at this stage.

These may be summarised as:

Overall: The company's broad marketing objective at this stage will be to protect and strengthen its position.

Product: The company will tighten its product line, deleting or making enhancements to weaker items and improving the quality of the whole range.

Price: The company's prices will match or beat those of competitors.

Promotion: The company's communication will be focused on building brand loyalty.

Distribution: The company will seek the strong support of its dealer network.

While strategy implications of PLC theory such as these can certainly provide a starting point for managers faced with tough competitive challenges, there are many who think that it is a limited and overly-simplistic tool, and that its use in industries (such as the computer industry) where entire life cycles are already short and becoming shorter because of the pace of technological change is inappropriate.

Those who reject PLC theory claim that product life cycle patterns are too variable to be typified, or that the duration of the stages are too unpredictable to be used as a basis of strategy. When, they ask, does the growth stage stop and the maturity stage begin? Is a product really in decline when the sales downturn begins, or is it just a temporary downturn?

Perhaps the harshest critics of PLC theory are those who say that a decline in a product's sales is not inevitable at all. They claim that it is because the company treats its products as if they will eventually decline that they do decline.

As suggested earlier, however, smart marketing practitioners do not fall for the trap of blindly following the PLC strategy guidelines. They use its implications merely as one more guide to strategy development, and as one more tool or technique against which to test their own intuitive judgements.

Chapter 3: Competitive Advantage and the Marketing Discipline

Fig. 3.4: Summary of PLC Objectives, Characteristics and Strategies

Product Life Cycle Stages	Introduction	Growth	Competitive Turbulence	Maturity	Decline
Marketing Objective	Create awareness; build primary demand	Foster selective demand	Protect market share	Manage for earnings	Reduce expenditure; prepare to exit market

Characteristics:

	Introduction	Growth	Competitive Turbulence	Maturity	Decline
Sales	Low	Rising rapidly	Slowing	At peak	Declining
Costs	High cost per customer	Average cost per customer	Falling cost per customer	Low cost per customer	Low cost per customer
Profits (per unit)	Negative	Rising to peak	Declining	Steady	Declining
Customers	Innovators	Early adopters	Early majority	Late majority	Laggards
Competitors	None	Growing number	Saturated; shakeout begins	Declining in number	Continuing decline

Strategies:

	Introduction	Growth	Competitive Turbulence	Maturity	Decline
Product	One version	Extensions to range	Product improvements	Full range	Retain best sellers only
Price	Skimming or penetration	Deal, discount to meet competitors	Deal, discount to meet competitors	Price to hold market share	Reduce; price to maintain margins
Promotion	Inform	Persuade	Persuade; stress differentiation	Remind	None
Place	Limited; patchy	Build channels of distribution	Seek strong support of dealers	Full coverage of market	Retain best outlets only

Endnotes

1. See Peter Drucker, *Management: Tasks, Responsibilities, Practices*, Harper & Row, New York, 1973, pp. 64-65.

2. Theodore Levitt, *The Marketing Imagination*, Free Press, New York, revised 1986.

3. For more information on "market battlefield mapping", see William Rothschild, *How to Gain and Maintain a Competitive Advantage*, McGraw Hill, New York, 1984.

4. See Michael E. Porter, *Competitive Advantage: Creating and Sustaining Superior Performance*, Free Press, New York, 1985.

5. See, for instance, Philip Kotler, *Marketing Management: Analysis, Planning, Implementation and Control*, Prentice Hall, Englewood Cliffs (1994) for a more detailed description of a marketing information system of this kind.

6. See Note 5 above. Again, Kotler's *Marketing Management* is a useful source of additional information.

7. C.R. Wasson, in *Dynamic Competitive Strategy and Product Life Cycles* (Challenge Books, 1974), and George S. Day, in *Analysis for Strategic Marketing Decisions (*West Publishing Company, 1986), have both provided adequate summaries of the general strategic implications of product life cycle theory, including the specific consideration of the competitive turbulence stage.

Chapter 3: Competitive Advantage and the Marketing Discipline

WHEN THE GOING GETS TOUGH ...

MAGAZINE WARS

The fierce competition among weekly women's magazines in recent years seems likely to continue for some time yet. At least one new title is being developed, new resources are being put behind a newcomer, and a former market leader is being given an overhaul to rejuvenate it.

The newcomer, to be launched next month by the teen-oriented Attic Futura (acquired last year by Pacific Magazines), is a local version of the British women's magazine, *Take a Break*. It is to be positioned as a rival to the big four of the local women's weekly magazine industry: *Woman's Day* and *New Weekly* (published by Australian Consolidated Press); *Who* (Time Warner) and *New Idea* (Pacific Magazines).

Take a Break will be Attic Futura's first grown-up title, but its proposed launch raises a number of questions. Is the market sound enough to sustain another new title? Can *Take a Break* be launched successfully without cannibalising *New Idea*, published by Attic Futura's parent?

Obviously, Pacific Magazines believes that it has the answer to these questions. But Australian Consolidated Press found that its *New Weekly* did not live up to its predicted level of sales when it was launched in 1993, and ACP is working hard right now to boost sales. But rival publishers believe that *New Weekly*'s losses will be at least $5 million in its first year. ACP admits that *New Weekly*'s sales have been disappointing but deny that its launch has been a disaster; sales of new magazines, they say, often need time to build up.

Pacific Magazines is taking no chances that its new entrant, *Take a Break*, will bite into sales of its *New Idea*, once the queen of the weekly women's magazines, but now running a poor second to ACP's *Woman's Day*. In its attempt to arrest its decline, Pacific Magazines has been tinkering with layouts and trying to make its editorial content brighter and more relevant.

New Idea recently published two editions in one week: one used the wedding of two TV soap stars as its cover story; the other the New South Wales bushfires. *New Idea* has also hired a new advertising agency and a new marketing director to beef up the title.

(Adapted from an article by Neil Shoebridge, "Media Buyers Say the Women's Magazine Market is Not as Elastic as Publishers Believe", *Business Review Weekly*, February 7, 1994.)

... THE TOUGH GET GOING

THE BATTLE FOR THE BODY

Elle Macpherson's success in Australia with her signature lingerie line (which was produced by the New Zealand-based Bendon company) has been spectacular. She is now gearing up to hit the U.S. market.

Now her success seems likely to be emulated, in the male segment of the underwear market, by a male model from New Zealand, John Andrews. Inspired by Macpherson's success, he has launched in New Zealand a line of men's athletic underwear, called BOD.

Andrews' idea to launch his own label was facilitated when the Calvin Klein range of athletic underwear arrived in New Zealand in September 1993. (The Calvin Klein label is produced in Australia by Davenport Industries which beat a swag of competitors for the Australasian licence.) Suddenly, the market for men's designer underwear opened up. Andrews considers his BOD range part of a new generation of men's underwear, which includes offerings from the Nikos line from Paris and that of former tennis ace, Bjorn Borg. All are striving to take on the Calvin Klein line which was originally launched in 1978.

"I see it as a huge market," says Andrews, who is also a presenter of New Zealand television's version of *Sale of the Century*. "I think there is an awareness of other brands out there now. Klein has been around for twenty years and it's had the market to itself."

BOD is being marketed, not just as an underwear product, but also as activewear. "Underwear is now worn to parties. There's no limit to where you can wear this product," says Andrews. BOD is also benefiting from exposure via the male strip ensemble, Manpower, which is BOD-outfitted for the cover of its 1995 calendar.

Andrews' BOD range is making inroads in Australia. Daimaru and Myer Melbourne have both picked up the range. Myer will be selling it from next month in its Sydney stores as well. Late last year, Andrews began exporting to Hong Kong. The influential U.S. retailers, Liberty House and Nordstrom, have also expressed some interest.

(Adapted from an article by Patty Huntington, "Pad the Parcel", *Age*, 25 February 1995, p.14.)

Chapter 3: Competitive Advantage and the Marketing Discipline

CASE STUDY 3:

KODAK: A NEW FOCUS

Eastman Kodak's new CEO, George Fisher, likes to point out the parallels between his strategy and that of the company's founder, George Eastman, who combined technological genius with something which has been in short supply at Kodak recently - marketing vision.

As this shows, Fisher doesn't lack self-confidence.

He left the CEO role at Motorola Inc. to take up the Kodak post. Although Kodak has spent billions on research and development and repeated restructurings, its earnings have been poor; it earned less in 1993 than it did in 1982. While it is blessed with a powerhouse brand name, it is trapped in a slow-growth industry, hobbled with huge debts and a dysfunctional management culture, and a dispirited workforce.

After less than a year in the position, Fisher has shaken up the sluggish giant. He has sold off its health-care business and refocused the company on to its core imaging business. He slashed debts from $7.5 billion in 1993 to $1.5 billion in 1994, and he has started to tackle the bloated management problem. University of Michigan's Professor C.K. Prahalad, who has been used by Kodak as a business consultant, says: "Fisher's first year has been a spectacular success. He has cleaned up the company and created a new spirit, a new willingness to compete."

But as Kodak now moves into the new era of digital imaging it faces powerful rivals. It will be going up against Fuji, Canon and Sony in such brutally competitive sectors of the market as printers and digital cameras. In its CD-ROM reading devices markets, it will compete with some very nimble manufacturers from Taiwan. In its computer peripherals markets, it will get hot competition from aggressive manufacturers from Singapore to Shanghai.

Outlining his strategy for these markets recently, Fisher said that he would continue to concentrate on the reform of company culture and costs. At the same time, he would focus on the basics, such as quality, customer needs, and shorter production development time. He thinks it will probably take three to five years before dramatic results are evident.

Fisher is convinced that its "golden goose", its consumer photography operation, can continue to grow steadily. This business contributes about 75% of the company's operating profit on just 42% of its revenue. He also expects the company's film and paper business to grow at 7% to 9% for the next decade. The anticipated growth in these two markets will support the expansion into new businesses and markets.

Fisher is very serious about expansion into Asia. He sees huge potential in China. He also sees vast untapped markets in Russia, India and Brazil. In fact, the company has already had a 400% growth in its businesses in Russia, admittedly from a small base, by franchising hundreds of Kodak Express minilabs and retail shops. In doing so, it has stolen a march on its major European rival, Agfa.

"Half the people in the world are yet to take their first photograph," says Fisher. "The opportunity is huge, and its nothing fancy. We just have to sell yellow boxes of film."

But geographic expansion is not the only strategy. This year, Kodak will re-launch its poorly-marketed "Photo CD" product, to make it more useful to millions of desktop PC users. Another promising new product is the CopyPrint station which uses digital technology to make enlargements from ordinary prints.

Progress with both of these new products has been slow to date, and some observers say that Fisher has taken on a monumental task at Kodak. But if anyone can force new products through the cumbersome consumer decision-making process, it is Fisher. At Motorola, he excelled at motivating people, pushing decision-making down, and picking up promising new technologies. At Kodak, he is emphasising cycle time, and has asked managers to set up measures. Before Fisher's arrival at Kodak, no one ever measured the time it took to complete projects or even how fast they were progressing.

All of this has caught the eye of Kodak's Japanese competitors, and one rival executive in Tokyo has commented that he thinks that Kodak might have a distinct competitive advantage in its "total market segment approach". While most Japanese competitors are developing scanners and peripherals, they are not part of an integrated whole. This, the Japanese executive thinks, could allow Kodak to set crucial industry standards. If, for instance, Kodak can make its Photo-CD a standard for the multimedia PC market, that could have big implications for competitors. "Kodak is a market leader," says the executive. "It's been in the imaging business longer than anyone."

However, even if it gets the technology right, a fundamental problem which Kodak (and Fisher) face is that Kodak has never been good at manufacturing electronic gear in high volumes at low cost. Nearly all of its gear is aimed at the less competitive, pricey, high end of the market.

Another big challenge will be to get "hot" new technologies around the world quickly. Kodak has always tended to concentrate on the U.S. market and to treat the rest of the world as an after-thought.

Nevertheless, Fisher relishes challenges like these. He finds them "invigorating". That's obvious - if he didn't, he would still be at Motorola.

(Adapted from an article by Mark Maremont, Margaret Dawson and Robert Neff, "Kodak's New Focus", *Business Week*, February 13, 1995.)

Chapter 3: Competitive Advantage and the Marketing Discipline

CASE STUDY - QUESTIONS FOR DISCUSSION

1. Who are Kodak's competitors? Discuss.

2. In its CD-ROM reading devices markets, Kodak will be "going up against some very nimble manufacturers in Taiwan". What competitive advantage(s) does Kodak have in that situation?

3. Kodak is a dominant market leader in its "consumer photography" operations. How might it be expected to act towards rivals?

4. Kodak is not a dominant leader in all of its markets. Does this mean it will have to play leader strategies in some markets, challenger strategies in others, and perhaps follower and/or nicher strategies in others? Is this possible? Discuss.

5. Kodak's CEO sees a huge opportunity for growth in the fact that "half of the people in the world have yet to take their first photograph". Do you agree with him? How does Kodak plan to capitalise on the opportunity it sees?

6. "If anyone can force new products through the cumbersome consumer decision-making process, it is Fisher." Discuss the consumer decision-making process, explaining whether you think it is "cumbersome"? How might Fisher attempt to "force" new products through the process?

7. At Kodak, George Fisher is focusing on "cycle time". What does this mean? How can a focus on "cycle time" confer a competitive advantage?

8. Kodak has "never been good at manufacturing electronic gear at low cost". What do you think it *has* it been good at?

9. "Another big challenge for Kodak will be to get its hot new technologies around the world quickly." Why is this a challenge? How might Kodak respond to the challenge?

10. What is meant by "a total segment approach"? How might this approach give Kodak a competitive advantage, as an executive from a rival company has suggested? (Consider this: Is Ferrari at a disadvantage in not taking a total segment approach in the automobile market? Is there a difference between its position and Kodak's?)

Competitive Advantage: Concepts and Cases

Michael E. Porter and Sustainable Competitive Advantage

In the matters of competitive strategy and competitive advantage, it is fair to say that no-one has had more influence than Professor Michael E. Porter of the Harvard Business School.

His views on how to compete first came to the attention of the world at large with the publication of his book, *Competitive Strategy: Techniques for Analyzing Industries and Competitors,* in 1980. The effect this book had on business thinking at the time, and has had since, has rightly been described as "explosive".[1] His second major book, *Competitive Advantage: Creating and Sustaining Superior Performance (* 1985), extended and expanded upon, his earlier treatment of the subject.

In these books, Porter makes three very valuable contributions to the body of thought on the ways in which a firm might develop a competitive advantage. These might be summarised as:

- industry structure analysis (or the "five forces" model)
- sources of sustainable competitive advantage (three generic strategies)
- the value chain concept

Industry Structure Analysis ("Five Forces" Model)

Porter believes that the nature and degree of competition in an industry hinge on five forces.

These five forces are:

- the threat of new entrants (or the presence or absence of barriers to entry)
- the bargaining power of buyers
- the bargaining power of suppliers
- the availability of substitute products
- the intensity of rivalry among the current industry competitors (or the jockeying for position).

According to Porter, the effect of these forces on the underlying economic structure of an industry will determine its profitability, and, as a consequence, the degree of competitiveness within it.

In order to be able to formulate strategies for dealing with these contending forces, a company must understand how they work in its industry and how they affect the company in its particular situation. These forces highlight the critical strengths and weaknesses of the company.

Competitive Advantage: Concepts and Cases

Understanding the forces, and being able to analyse the sources of the pressure that each force is able to bring to bear, is critical to being able to compete successfully in the industry.

Let us consider each of these five forces in turn.

Threat of New Entrants

If the barriers to entry to an industry are *low,* new competitors are likely to want to participate.

New entrants bring new capacity into the industry (that is, the ability to increase the volume and availability of the industry's product). They bring with them, too, a desire to gain market share. They often also bring with them substantial resources.

This means that the easier it is to enter an industry, the less profitable that industry is likely to be for the existing players.

If, on the other hand, there are *high* barriers to entry, or if any potential entrant can expect sharp retaliation from the existing competitors, new players will be less likely to want to participate.

There are a number of significant barriers to entry. They include:

Economies of scale
Competitors which can produce their product in large volumes are able to produce them more cheaply; the unit cost of production will be lower. Thus, they enjoy what is referred to as economies of scale.

Economies of scale deter entry by forcing any new player to come in on a large scale or to accept a cost disadvantage. Such economies may occur in financing, research and development, manufacturing, distribution, marketing, advertising ands sales promotion, utilisation of the sales force, service, and, in fact, in nearly every part of the business.

Product differentiation
Product differentiation is usually created by the building of strong brands.

Strong brands create a barrier to entry because they force potential new entrants to spend heavily to overcome existing brand loyalty. Advertising, customer service, being first into the industry, and product superiority all contribute to brand loyalty.

Capital requirements
Large sums of money are often required to enter an industry on a sufficiently large scale to make profits.

The need to invest the large sums required in order to compete effectively creates a barrier to entry, particularly if the capital is required for unrecoverable expenses such as up-front advertising or research and development.

Cost disadvantages regardless of size

The existing players in an industry usually have cost advantages which are not available to potential rivals, no matter what their size and resources.

The sources of these advantages may be many, but include those such as the effects of experience in the industry (the learning curve), patents and/or propriety technology, easier access to raw materials, assets purchased earlier at costs which are much higher later, government subsidies, and more favourable locations.

Access to distribution barriers

Often, the existing players have secured reliable distribution channels that a new entrant may find hard to break into, especially if there are few available channels.

Sometimes this barrier to entry is so high that a new entrant will have to create its own distribution channels if it wishes to participate.

Government policy

Governments can limit the number of players in an industry or even prevent new entrants from participating at all.

Government controls on air and water pollution standards or on safety regulations and the like can often be a deterrent to entry.

Bargaining Power of Buyers

When the buyers of an industry's products are powerful (that is, when they have high bargaining power), the profits to be made by each competitor are severely diminished. This may lead to increased competition for market share.

There are a number of conditions which will lead to the bargaining power of a customer group being *high*. They include the following:

There are only a few, large buyers:

If there are only a few, large buyers, the industry rivals are likely to have no alternative but to sell their product at the prices and terms which the large buyers dictate.

The products of the competitors in the industry are of a commodity nature (or incapable of being differentiated):

If the product of the industry rivals is of a commodity nature (that is, they are incapable of being differentiated), the bargaining power of the buyers is strengthened because no rival has anything special or superior with which to bargain for customer loyalty, a better price or better terms.

The products of the competitors in the industry are a significant component of the buyers' product:

If the product of the industry rivals is a significant component of the buyers' products, they will represent a large part of the buyers' costs. Thus, the buyers will be forever looking for ways to exert pressure on the industry rivals and so reduce their own costs.

The buying groups earn low profits:

If the buyers of the product of the industry rivals usually earn low profits, there is a great incentive for them to lower their purchasing costs. Thus, they will always be exerting pressure on the rivals to lower the price of their products.

The industry's product is unimportant to the quality of the buyers' products:

If the product of the industry rivals is not important to the quality of the buyers' finished products, the buyers' will not be prepared to pay as much for it as if the quality were important.

The industry's product does not save the buyers money:

If the product of the industry rivals saves the buyers some money, the buyers will want badly to have it. However, if the product does not save them money they will be less likely to seek it out eagerly or to pay heavily for it.

The buyers pose a credible threat of integrating backward and making the competitors' product themselves:

The bargaining power of the buyers is strengthened if the industry rivals believe that there is a real risk that the buyers might integrate backwards (that is, purchase a company which makes the product of the industry rivals and so have their own ready supply of the product.)

Bargaining Power Of Suppliers

When the suppliers to an industry are powerful (that is, they have high bargaining power), they can exert pressure on the competitors by raising their prices or reducing the quality of the purchased goods and/or services.

There are a number of factors which contribute to the *high* bargaining power of a supplier group. They include:

There are only a few, large suppliers:

If there are only a few suppliers, their bargaining power will be higher because the industry rivals will have less choice in the matter of supply.

The suppliers' product is unique, or highly differentiated:

If the suppliers' product is unique or highly differentiated, the industry rivals are in a weak bargaining position if they have no choice but to buy the product.

The suppliers' product does not have to contend with other products for sale to the industry:

If the suppliers' product does not have to contend with other products (that is, if it is the only product the industry rivals purchases in significant quantity), the bargaining power of the suppliers is stronger because the industry rivals are likely to be less concerned with reducing the cost of the product.

Chapter 4: Michael E. Porter and Sustainable Competitive Advantage

The suppliers pose a credible threat of integrating forward into the industry's business:

The bargaining power of the suppliers is strengthened if the industry rivals believe that there is a real risk that the suppliers might integrate forward (that is, purchase a company which makes the product of the industry rivals and so have a ready outlet for their own product.)

The competitors are not important customers of the supplier group:

If the suppliers do not consider the industry rivals as a group to be important customers (in terms of their size and the volumes they purchase), the bargaining power of the suppliers will be high.

Availability of Substitutes

Substitutes are those products which are quite different in form but which offer a real alternative to the industry competitors' products. For example, the use of some forms of plastic can be substituted for steel in the building industry.

The ready availability of substitute products can limit the profit potential of competitors in an industry by placing a ceiling on the prices they can charge.

Unless the industry competitors can make their product significantly superior in the eyes of their customers, or differentiate it somehow (by marketing or distribution, for instance), the industry competitors will suffer in earnings and possibly in growth.

Buyers are more likely to turn to substitutes in conditions such as these:

The substitute is close in price and performance to the industry's product:

If buyers are able to perceive no significant difference between the price and performance of the product of the industry rivals and the price and performance of a readily available substitute, they are not likely to remain loyal to the products of the industry rivals.

The switching costs are low:

Sometimes, buyers are reluctant to switch to a substitute because the switching costs (the costs in terms of the time and effort involved in making the switch from one product to another) are high. However, if the switching costs are not high, the likelihood of buyers turning to substitutes increases.

The buyers have been accustomed to making switches to alternative products in the past:

If buyers are already in the habit of switching from one product to another, they are more likely to be attracted from the product of an industry rival to a substitute product if one is, or becomes, available.

The Intensity of Rivalry

The rivalry among existing competitors, or the jockeying for position among them, can be either intense or placid.

Intense rivalry is exhibited in an industry in tactics like price-cutting, new product innovations and heavy bouts of "knock-out", comparative advertising.

There are a number of conditions which contribute to *intense rivalry*. They include:

The competitors are numerous, or are roughly equal in size and power:

If there are many competitors fighting to hold their place in the industry, the rivalry is likely to be more intense than if there are only a few; a few competitors may manage to co-exist in relative harmony. Similarly, if the competitors are relatively equal in size and strength, the battles between them may be fiercer; if some are much larger than others, the smaller ones may be unwilling to engage in bitter market share wars.

The industry growth is slow:

Slow growth in an industry is likely to mean that the rivals will have difficulty in meeting the targets expected of them by stakeholders. This may precipitate intense battles for additional market share.

The industry's product lacks differentiation or switching costs:

Differentiated products and high switching costs lock in buyers and protect an individual competitor from raids on its customer base by rivals.

The fixed costs are high:

If a competitor's fixed costs are high there is a tendency for it to reduce its prices in order to lift its revenue. In reducing its prices, it puts pressure on its industry rivals.

The product is perishable:

A perishable product creates strong pressure to reduce prices. When any competitor reduces prices, it intensifies industry rivalries.

The exit barriers are high:

If it is difficult for a competitor to sell out, or to walk away from its investment, the intensity of rivalry is likely to be increased.

The rivals are diverse in strategies, origins and "personalities".

If the industry rivals are diverse in strategies, origins and "personalities" there is likely to be more intense rivalry than if they follow similar strategies and have similarities in origins and "personalities".

The Five Forces Model Illustrated

Porter has illustrated the way in which these "five forces" affect all competitors in an industry.[2] He takes the case of the U.S. pharmaceutical industry as an example.

Until the middle of the 1980s, he says, being a player in the giant pharmaceutical industry in the U.S. was like having a licence to print money. Every competitor made very substantial profits year after year.

Why was this so?

Chapter 4: Michael E. Porter and Sustainable Competitive Advantage

The answer, according to Porter, is that the five forces were favourable to the players in the industry:

The *barriers to entry were high*. To enter the industry required the investment of many millions of dollars (mainly to be used in the development and testing of new drugs and the establishment of a sales force large enough to bring these drugs to the attention of the doctors who would prescribe them). Very few new companies could afford the huge investment required. Therefore, this force was *favourable* to the entrenched competitors.

The *bargaining power of customers was low*. Doctors had little choice but to prescribe the products of the companies in the industry; their patients had little choice but to buy them. This force was also *favourable* to the competitors in the industry.

The *bargaining power of suppliers was low*. The ingredients used to manufacture the drugs were cheap and readily available from many sources. This force was also *favourable* to the industry competitors.

There were *no ready substitutes* for the drugs. If a patient required a particular drug, he or she had to have it. There were no adequate substitutes. This force, too, was *favourable* to the industry competitors.

And, finally, *the rivalry between competitors was not intense*. Rather, it was of a "gentlemanly" nature. Many manufacturers' drugs were protected by patent, or were serving markets that other manufacturers had not entered. There was no need for the rivals to engage in bitter and profit-reducing price wars, or to "slug it out" in costly promotional battles. Again, this force was *favourable*.

Thus, says Porter, the U.S. pharmaceutical industry was a "five-star" industry for twenty or more years. Every competitor made profits of a magnitude that were the envy of competitors in nearly every other industry.

By the end of the 1980s, however, things had begun to change. By that time, three of the five forces had become *unfavourable*.

First, the barriers to entry had been lowered. Advancements in biotechnology had significantly lowered the cost of producing new drugs, and entry to the industry required a far smaller capital outlay.

Second, substitutes had begun to appear - in the form of generics. Because the patents over many of the drugs of the entrenched competitors had expired, their drugs could now be manufactured by other competitors also. In other words, many of the drugs to which entrenched competitors once had sole rights were now available from other companies as well.

Third, the bargaining power of buyers had increased. This was because the U.S. government had legislated to require doctors to prescribe a cheaper generic drug, if one were available, in preference to the more expensive proprietary items. This legislation also made it harder for patients to recover their full payments for medicinal drugs from their medical benefits societies unless a generic drug had been subscribed by their doctor.

As a result of these three economic forces becoming *unfavourable* to rivals in the industry, it had become a much less profitable industry than it had been earlier. As a result of this, the competition between the major players began to intensify.

For Porter, therefore, industry structure analysis using the "five forces" model has three purposes:

- a company can use it to assess the likely profitability of an industry before deciding to enter it. (Note that the model can be applied to a market or a segment of the market in just the same way as it can be applied to an industry.)

- a company which is already in the industry can use it periodically to assess whether any structural changes have occurred since it entered it.

- a company can use it to guide its competitive strategy formulation. Its strategy ought to be directed, primarily, at the forces which are presently unfavourable.

Examples of the way in which a company might formulate strategy to offset unfavourable forces include:

- investing in the building of strong brand in order to raise the barriers to entry by the creation of customer loyalty, thus making it difficult for any potential new competitor to get a foothold in the industry.

- forging strategic alliances with suppliers and distributors in order to raise the barriers to entry by blocking access to key materials or to important distribution channels.

- creating strong relationships with suppliers, distributors, customers, governments and all other influential groups to ward off any threat posed by the availability of substitute products.

- integrating backwards to negate the high bargaining power of suppliers or forwards to negate the high bargaining power of buying groups.

Sources of Sustainable Competitive Advantage - and the Three Generic Strategies

Having discussed the way in which his "five forces" model can be used to assess the likely profitability (or unprofitablility) of an industry, Porter points out that in every industry - whether the contending five forces are favourable or unfavourable - some firms, year in and year out, seem to be able to be more profitable than others.

Why is that?

It is, says Porter, because they have a *sustainable* competitive advantage over their rivals.

This idea brings us to his second important contribution the field of competitive strategy: his notion that there are, fundamentally, only two sources of sustainable competitive advantage.

Chapter 4: Michael E. Porter and Sustainable Competitive Advantage

The Idea of "Sustainable" Competitive Advantage

But it is important to note what Porter means by the word "sustainable".

Any competitor might get a short-term advantage over any of its rivals in many ways - by lowering its prices, or by an advertising campaign, or by some form of sales promotion, for example. But these forms of competitive advantage are not sustainable, because they can be easily copied, or even improved upon, by competitors. Thus, the competitive advantage they give will only be temporary.

"Sustainable" competitive advantage is the kind of advantage which can not be easily copied. It is an advantage which is long-term, and which cannot be easily eroded by the activities of competitors.

For Porter, there are only *two* sources of this kind of long-term, not-easily-eroded sustainable competitive advantage:

- *low cost,* and
- *differentiation.*

The Low Cost Advantage

The *low cost advantage* is obtained when a particular firm is able to produce and market its product at a significantly lower cost than its competitors. It is usually the planned result of policies aimed at achieving economies of scale and managing away costs.

(Be careful not to confuse "low cost" with "low price"; the low cost producer does not *necessarily* sell its product at a lower price.)

To implement a low cost strategy effectively, a firm generally requires tight cost control and frequent, detailed expenditure control reports. The low cost competitor is characterised by a tightly structured organisation with well-defined managerial responsibilities. Often, incentives are provided to managers who meet strict quantitative targets.

In addition the firm also requires particular skills and resources, including:

Sustained capital investment and access to capital:

The low cost strategy requires sustained capital investment and access to capital because high volumes of production and broad market coverage are necessary if economies of scale are to be achieved.

Process engineering skills:

The low cost strategy requires the firm to have a high level of process engineering skills because the firm must be able to manufacture its product quickly and economically.

Intensive supervision of labour:

The low cost strategy requires intensive supervision of labour in order to minimise wastage of time and materials.

A product designed for ease of manufacture:

The low cost strategy requires the firm to have a "no frills" product that can be produced rapidly and economically.

The low cost competitor (or *cost leader*) in an industry has great advantages:

- because its margins are greater, it has more profit to plough back into research and development, or product innovation, or marketing, or to use in any other way to further improve its position.

- because its margins are greater, it can, if necessary, withstand a price war with its competitors.

Cost leadership also provides a defence against each of the "five forces":

Entry barriers:

A low cost advantage inhibits the likelihood of any new entrant, unless it can match the cost leader's cost advantage.

Bargaining power of buyers:

A low cost advantage prevents a buying group from driving drive down prices beyond the level of price set by the next most efficient (next lowest cost) competitor.

Bargaining power of suppliers:

A low cost advantage provides the flexibility to cope with price increases from suppliers.

Threat of substitutes:

A low cost advantage places the firm in the position of being less threatened by lower-priced substitutes than any other competitor.

Jockeying for position among industry rivals:

A low cost advantage enables the firm to withstand competitors' price wars; the low cost firm can still remain profitable when its rivals have eliminated their margins through discounting and price competition.

The Differentiation Advantage

A differentiation advantage is obtained when a firm is able to charge a premium price for its product (that is, a price significantly higher than that of its competitors) and still retain its customer base.

The offering of the firm is perceived by buyers to be uniquely different - in ways that are of value to them - from the offerings of competitors.

Chapter 4: Michael E. Porter and Sustainable Competitive Advantage

Differentiation can take many forms. For instance, it might be based on uniqueness in product design or features, on product quality, on brand image, on customer service, on more convenient locations or on the number of outlets. In fact, in an ideal sense, it will be based on a combination of factors which the customers perceive to be unique, different and more valuable to them.

To implement a differentiation strategy effectively, a firm generally requires strong co-ordination among functions such as R & D, product development and marketing; facilities to attract highly skilled and creative people and a company culture to retain them; and incentives based on subjective measures rather than on the meeting of strict quantitative targets.

In addition the firm also requires particular skills and resources, including:

Strong marketing capabilities:

The differentiation strategy is sometimes referred to as the "marketing" strategy. Because the product will be sold to customers at a premium price, the "extra value" it represents will need to be provided.

Product engineering skills:

Unlike the low cost strategy which requires *process* engineering skills to ensure cheapness in production, the differentiation strategy requires high-level *product* engineering skills. The product offering must be seen as superior enough to warrant a premium price.

Creative flair:

The provision of a product that can attract a premium price will require a high level of creativity.

Strong capability in basic research:

The differentiator must have a very thorough understanding of the needs and wants of customers and to be able to produce innovative offerings to meet them. This kind of innovation calls for a strong capability in basic research.

Corporate reputation for quality and/or technological leadership:

The differentiation strategy generally requires the firm to have a reputation for quality and/or technological superiority. It is unlikely that the products of a firm without this kind of reputation will command a premium price.

Long tradition in the business:

To command a premium price for its offering, the firm may need the trust and loyalty of its customers. The creation of loyalty and trust of this kind may require a long tradition in the business.

Strong cooperation from the channels of distribution:

The differentiation strategy may require the strong cooperation of the channels of distribution, especially if the point of differentiation is availability, speed, reliability, freshness, and so on.

Competitive Advantage: Concepts and Cases

A differentiation advantage also offers a defence against the *unfavourable* effects of the five forces, but in different ways to cost leadership:

Entry barriers:

The differentiator creates strong brand loyalty. This requires any potential new entrant to overcome the "uniqueness" provide entry barriers.

Bargaining power of buyers:

The differentiator's buyers are less price sensitive because they have no comparable alternatives.

Bargaining power of suppliers:

The differentiator yields higher margins to offset any price increases by suppliers.

Threat of substitutes:

The differentiator, having achieved strong brand loyalty, places itself in the position of being less threatened by lower-priced substitutes than any other competitor.

Jockeying for position among rivals in the industry:

The differentiator insulates itself from rivalry by using brand loyalty to lower customers' price sensitivity.

Both the cost leadership strategy and the differentiation strategy enable a firm to make greater-than-average profits in its industry. This allows it a greater margin to plough back into the skills and assets required to further reduce its costs, or to further enhance its differentiation - the source of its competitive advantage in the first place.

Competitive Scope

To understand how both the low cost advantage and the differentiation work in practice, Porter introduces the idea of *competitive scope*.

A cost leadership advantage may be pursued across broad market sectors or across narrow market sectors.

Similarly, a differentiation advantage may be pursued across broad market sectors or across narrow market sectors.

If a certain competitor attempts to capture industry-wide markets its competitive scope is *broad*. It will produce in large volumes, attracting as many buyers as possible.

If, on the other hand, it targets only particular market segments its competitive scope is *narrow*. These segments may be based on geographic, or demographic, or psychographic or behavioural variables. Wanting only to serve a smaller part of the market, it will produce in much smaller volumes.

Chapter 4: Michael E. Porter and Sustainable Competitive Advantage

The notion of competitive scope leads Porter to suggest that there are *three generic strategies* for competitive advantage. By the term "generic", Porter means strategies which are basic or fundamental and upon which the firm's other strategies and tactics will be built.

Three Generic Strategies

Porter's three generic strategies are:

    i.   Cost Leadership

    ii.   Differentiation

    iii. Focus

Cost Leadership

Here, a firm seeks to be the cost leader, pursuing the advantage this strategy confers across broad markets and attracting as many customers as possible.

Porter has used the example of one of Proctor and Gamble's operating divisions, Ivory Soap, to illustrate the cost leadership advantage.

"Ivory" soap is marketed as a "no-frills" product. Although it is a plain soap, it is a good, honest product with broad market appeal. It has equal attraction to men and women, old and young, families and singles. It sells in large volumes. Because it contains a lot of "air bubbles", which means it contains less material, it is cheap to manufacture. It contains no expensive additives (such as those in the soaps of some of its competitors: "Dial" with its deodorisers, and "Dove" with its skin creams.) It is plainly packaged. Because it is an old, well-established brand in the market, it requires comparatively little advertising support. Although it is usually cheaper than competing soaps, its price is kept high enough for the Ivory Division of Proctor and Gamble to achieve greater-than-average profit margins in the soap industry. These above average margins allow it to withstand price wars when they occur, and to sink money back into new processes and technologies to further increase the cost advantage it already has.

Differentiation

Here, a firm seeks to be differentiated, pursuing the advantage this strategy confers across broad markets and attracting as many customers as possible.

Porter has used the example of American Airlines to illustrate the differentiation advantage.

American Airlines competes in the very crowded, and often cut-throat, U.S. domestic airline market. Although its standard fares are usually significantly higher than those of competitors, it attracts a large volume of passengers of all kinds - business travellers, holiday makers, people visiting friends and relatives and so on. It has broad market appeal. It is able to attract a very large customer base, despite its higher fares because it offers things that customers perceive to valuable - and worth the extra cost. For instance, its planes have more comfortable seats and greater leg-room. Its planes are more likely than competitors' to take off and arrive on time. The on-board food and services are superior. More importantly, it does not over-book its flights to the extent that other airlines do, and so there is less chance that passengers will be "bumped" (unable to board the plane because it is over-booked).

Being able to charge a premium price for these services which are perceived by customers to be "different" and valuable allows American Airlines to achieve greater-than-average profits. It can withstand price wars, and it can plough back some of its profit into enhancing those differentiated features from which its competitive advantage arises in the first place.

Focus

Here, a firm seeks to focus on a part of the market only, pursuing the advantage this strategy confers in a narrow market sector. Note that a focus player may choose to pursue its advantage by a *focus on cost* or a *focus on differentiation*. A firm which employs a *cost focus* attempts to concentrate on serving a segment whose needs are less than average. A firm which employs a *differentiation focus* attempts to concentrate an serving a segment whose needs are greater than average.

Porter has used the example of La Quinta, a U.S. motel chain to illustrate the cost focus advantage.

La Quinta does not target broad markets. It focuses on one segment of the market - the business traveller. It is not particularly concerned with the needs and wants of other users of motels. For this reason, there are no swimming pools, no restaurants, no room service and no fancy lobbies in La Quinta motels, because it believes that these features are not important to its targeted group. It does, however, provide all of those things which *are* of great importance to its targeted group. Its rooms are very quiet so that the tired business traveller can relax and sleep. It has telephones, fax machines, newspapers and all the usual requirements of busy business people. In doing away with unimportant features, it keeps its costs low and it passes the savings back to its customers in the form of lower prices.

In ways such as this, La Quinta has made greater-than-average profits in its industry. These greater margins can be used to further enhance its cost focus advantage.

Porter has used the example of Cray Research, a U.S. manufacturer of supercomputers, to illustrate the cost differentiation advantage.

Cray Research focuses on a very narrow segment of the computer industry. It makes the world's most powerful computer, the Cray. As each computer costs about $15 million to buy, Cray knows that its product has only narrow appeal. Cray computers are primarily made for very big and specialised applications; they are, for instance, used for military purposes by the U.S. armed services. Each computer is hand made. Although the amount of "down-time" to service them is minimal, each comes with a full complement of spare parts. Two of Cray's own people are also supplied to each customer, free for a year or more, to train the customer's people in the use of the Cray.

Those who buy a Cray computer are prepared to pay a premium price for the specialised equipment and services they get - and value. This allows Cray to make greater-than-average profits in its industry, profits which can be used to reinvest into assets and skills to further enhance its already-significant differentiation focus advantage.

Chapter 4: Michael E. Porter and Sustainable Competitive Advantage

A Note on Porter's Examples

Porter's examples - Ivory Soap, American Airlines, La Quinta and Cray Research - have drawn a great deal of criticism. Some people have pointed out that, in some respects, they are no longer valid. Cray Research, for instance, no longer focuses on the supercomputer as its only product; it has changed it focus differentiation strategy and now targets broader markets with an expanded product range.

This, however, does not invalidate Porter's generic strategy idea. After all, we live in dynamic and hostile times, and if a firm's competitive environment alters drastically it will have to change its strategies from time to time if it is to survive.

In fact, Porter himself has made that very point. In his "Ivory" soap example, he makes it clear that Ivory, for most of its 120-year history, did not pursue a cost leadership strategy but a differentiation strategy. It was only in the 1950s and 1960s, when the even more highly differentiated brands, "Dial" and "Dove", began to compete strongly with Ivory in its traditional markets, that Proctor and Gamble decided to change Ivory's strategic direction.

At that time, Proctor and Gamble's management had two options: either to add expensive ingredients to Ivory to enable it to "out-gun" Dial and Dove on unique and differentiated features, or not to add these ingredients and to go for cost leadership. It chose the latter course of action, but at the same time created a new brand to compete in the premium-price segment of the market with the two newcomers.

In all, it seems fairer to Porter to take his examples simply as that - contemporary illustrations his generic strategies in action. If the firms he has chosen no longer use the strategy, or even if they no are longer making greater-than-average profits, they are useful examples of what he wanted to convey. There may be many other reasons for the poor execution of the strategies or for a change of strategic direction.

"Stuck-in-the-Middle"

Porter believes that all firms can be "winners" in their chosen industries if they pursue any *one* of these three generic strategies - *cost leadership, differentiation,* or *focus* - single-mindedly.

However, the firm must be *single-minded*. It must be crystal clear about which *one* of the strategies it is following. To pursue two strategic directions at the one time can be a strategy fraught with danger, says Porter.

The pursuit of low cost requires a different managerial mind-set and different skills and assets than the pursuit of differentiation. To pursue both at the same time is risky. The danger is that the firm will get "stuck-in-the-middle".

A "stuck-in-the-middle" strategy will not achieve any competitive advantage, and the firm will be a "loser" in its industry.

Is Being "Stuck-in-the-Middle" Inevitable?

Perhaps nothing has been more contentious in all of Porter's valuable work, however, than this notion that, to compete successfully, a company must select one or other of the three generic strategies outlined above and pursue it single-mindedly.

While some support for this idea is to be found in the empirical testing of researchers - see, for instance, the studies by Dess and Davies (1984), McNamee and McHugh (1984), Miller and Friesen (1986) and White (1986) - it has been roundly criticised in the theoretical contributions of Karnani (1984), Murray (1988), Hill (1988), Hendry (1990), Cronshaw, Davis and Kay (1990) and Faulkner and Bowman (1990).[3]

Most of the latter group argue that a firm can, in fact, pursue a low cost and a differentiation strategy simultaneously. They reject Porter's "stuck-in-the-middle" notion. But, in doing so, they may overlook the fact that Porter is talking about the *risk* of being "stuck-in-the-middle", not the inevitability of it.

Linden Brown, in his *Competitive Marketing Strategy* (1989), draws upon the work of the U.K. academic and marketing planning authority, Malcolm McDonald, to illustrate the case of two firms which are highly differentiated and, at the same time, enjoy cost leadership positions in their respective industries.[4]

In the fast-food industry, says Brown, McDonald's is a highly differentiated cost leader. But it achieved this position in its market not by the pursuit of both strategies simultaneously but by going first in one direction and then in the other.

McDonald's started out in a *commodity* position. That is, it was not the highly differentiated fast-food outlet it is today. It had only low coverage of the market and so its costs per unit were relatively high.

First, it concentrated on improving its differentiation. Its strategy was to make itself distinctive in its market by adding products and services that were "different" and highly valued by its customers.

Then, having achieved this, it began to broaden its competitive scope, seeking greater market coverage in order to achieve scale economies. Concentrating also on technological improvements to lower costs, it attained its present cost leadership with differentiation position.

Brown uses the case of the BIC company to illustrate a different route to the cost leadership with high differentiation position.

Like McDonald's, BIC started in a *commodity* position. First, its strategy was to broaden its competitive scope to achieve scale economies and lower costs. In this way, it achieved a *cost leadership* position - low cost, low differentiation, high coverage of the market. Next, it broadened its range, adding different and valued products to its line, to achieve its present position of highly differentiated cost leader.

Chapter 4: Michael E. Porter and Sustainable Competitive Advantage

Risks of the Generic Strategies

The danger of "being stuck-in-the-middle" is not the only risk involved in giving practical application to the three generic strategies. Porter acknowledges several other risks of each generic strategy.

The risks associated with a *cost leadership* strategy include:
- the technological superiority which provides a low cost to a manufacturer might be lost if the technology of the industry changes.
- a cost advantage might be diminished by competitors who simply copy what the low cost player has learnt through years of experience.
- a cost advantage might be lost if, in seeking to reduce cost further, the low cost player ignores product quality and marketing.
- a low cost advantage might disappear if costs rise to the point where the price of the product has to be raised to a level which gets too close to the differentiator's price.

The risks associated with a *differentiation* strategy include:
- the premium price required to offset the cost of adding valuable features might become too high in the eyes of the customers.
- the customers' perceptions of what is "valuable" might change at any time.
- by imitating the features of the differentiator's offering, other manufacturers might narrow the perceived customer value.

The risks associated with a *focus* strategy include:
- the broad cost leader might achieve lower costs than the cost focus competitor and so attracts its customers.
- the broad differentiator might achieve more differentiation than the differentiation focus competitor and so attracts its customers.
- the gap between what the customer perceives to be valuable in the focus player's offering and what the broad market player offers might get narrower.
- other focus players (those with an even narrower focus) might out-focus the focuser.

The Value Chain Concept

Porter's third major contribution to the field of competitive advantage is the *value chain* concept.

He believes that every aspect of a firm's operations is designed to add "value" to its offering in the eyes of the customer. This "value" may be extended to customers in terms of lower prices or additional benefits.

What a firm must be able to do, therefore, is to cut out of its operations any activity or expense that adds unnecessarily to its cost, while at the same time building value in terms of increasing the appeal its offering has to its customers.

Competitive Advantage: Concepts and Cases

To assist in this regard, Porter provides a tool (which he refers to as a "disaggregating" tool) which allows the firm to break down its value activities into small pieces so that each can be closely examined for their strategic relevance in adding value or reducing cost.

Value Activities

According to Porter, it is helpful to think of the firm's value chain as consisting of nine *value activities*. Five of these are *primary activities* and four are *support activities*.

Each of these activities is strategically relevant in generating the revenue a firm receives, but each also adds to its costs. The difference between the revenue received and the cost of producing the revenue is the firm's margin.

The five primary activities are:

Inbound logistics:

The taking delivery of, transport, storage and handling of inputs to the product which the firm manufactures.

Operations:

The transformation or manufacturing of the inputs into finished products.

Outbound logistics:

The storage, handling, transport and delivery of the firms finished product to distributors and/or end users.

Marketing and sales:

The activities such as marketing management, advertising, sales promotion, personal selling, sales force administration, public relations and so on which are involved in persuading buyers to purchase the finished product and making it possible for them to do so.

Service:

The activities involved in the provision of services such as installation, training, maintenance, warranty, repair and so on which enhance or maintain the value of the product.

The four support (or secondary) activities are:

The firm's infrastructure:

The activities which include general management and planning, accounting and finance, the provision of legal services, quality management and so on. These activities usually support the whole value chain.

Human resources management:

The activities involved in the recruitment, selection, deployment, training, development and compensation of all types of personnel.

Chapter 4: Michael E. Porter and Sustainable Competitive Advantage

Technology development:

The activities involved in the use and development of information technology and process equipment.

Procurement:

The activities involved in the procurement or purchasing of the wide variety of inputs required throughout the firm.

Value Activity Labels

In reviewing these nine value activities it should be noted that Porter believes that value activity labels are arbitrary. That is, he believes that in managers should be free to label their own value chain activities to suit themselves. What is important is that whatever value activity labels are used should be those that provide the clearest insights into the business.

Similarly, he believes that the sequence in which they are illustrated and examined is unimportant. What is important is that the order chosen should enhance the intuitive clarity of the value chain for the managers.

Disaggregation of the Value Activities

Using the value chain tool, a firm can display its "total value" - that is, it can examine closely what value is created at each stage, what the cost of each activity is and what its total margin is. It can then work on adding value or reducing costs in ways that will enhance the margin.

Each value activity can be further disaggregated or sub-divided.

That is, the "Inbound Logistics" activity could be further disaggregated into the separate elements of which it consists: inwards transport, inbound materials inspection, raw materials inventory, raw materials storage, raw materials handling, for instance, to allow for a closer examination of cost-reduction and value-creation opportunities. Similarly, the "Marketing and Sales" activity could be further disaggregated into the separate elements of which it consists: marketing management, advertising, sales force administration, sales force operations, technical literature and sales promotions, for instance, for the same reason.[5]

In brief, the value chain is a tool to be used in the identification of the elements of the business in which a company creates value for its customers. In Figure 5.8, Porter shows the cost drivers in the value chain of a consumer durables manufacturing firm. Here, the manufacturer attempts to identify the separate elements which contribute significantly to its costs. This is a necessary first step in its attempt to achieve lower costs without decreasing the value it creates for customers.[6]

Thus, the important thing is that the firm must be careful not to cut costs in any way that weakens or disrupts the value it adds to its customers. Its task is to drive cost out of its business in areas where it can be done without destroying value.

While this sounds fairly straightforward, Porter warns of the *linkages* that exist between one value activity and another. These linkages mean that a firm might unwittingly weaken itself by chopping cost in one *seemingly* unimportant area (as far as adding customer value goes) without perceiving that it is linked to some other area which is also weakened in the process.

For example, in attempting to cut costs a firm might examine its inbound logistics area. Suppose that in doing so it identifies its pallet storage area as one which is costly to maintain. It decides to reduce drastically the number of pallets it keeps on hand. Now, suppose that the day after it discards its excess pallets it gets in a very big order from a key customer and is delayed in filling the order because it has not got sufficient pallets on hand. In this case, the company might not have properly understood the linkage between a seemingly unimportant matter (from the customer's point of view) of pallet storage and its sales and marketing function.

Porter also stresses the linkages which exist in the value chains of all firms in the supply chain. To a large extent, a competitor in any industry depends on its suppliers and distributors in its attempt to create value for its customers; if its suppliers and/or distributors let it down, it will let its customers down. He emphasises the need for firms to look for competitive advantages beyond its own value chain, to examine the value chains of their suppliers and distributors, as well as their own, in an endeavour to deliver its offering in the most favourable way to its customers.

This implies the necessity of the firm to understand the linkages between its own value activities, its suppliers' value activities and its distributors' value activities and to work with these supply and distribution partners to deliver value to the end user.

Endnotes

1. See John I. Moore, *Writers on Strategy and Strategic Management*, Penguin Books, London, 1992, pp.42-45.

2. See Porter, M.E., "How Competitive Forces Shape Strategy":, *Harvard Business Review*, March-April 1979. See also Porter, M.E., *Competitive Strategy: Techniques for Analyzing Industries and Competitors*, Free Press, New York, 1980 and Porter, M.E., *Competitive Advantage: Creating and Sustaining Superior Performance*, Free Press, New York, 1985. Porter has also explained his industry structure model and three generic strategies in a videotape series produced by the Harvard Business School.

3. Dess, G.G. and Davis, P.S., "Porter's Generic Strategies as Determinants of Strategic Group Membership and Organisation Performance", *Academy of Management Journal*, Vol.27, No.3, 1984, pp.467-488; McNamee, P. and McHugh, M, "Competitive Strategies in the Clothing Industry", *Long Range Planning*, Vol.22, No.4, 1989, pp.63-71; Miller, D. and Friesen, P.H., "Porter's Generic Strategies and Performance: an Empirical Examination with American Data (Part 2: Performance Implications", *Organisation Studies,* Vol7. No.3, 1986, pp.255-261; White, R.E., "Generic Business Strategies, Organisational Context and Performance: an Empirical Investigation", *Strategic Management Journal*, Vol.7, 1986, pp.217-231; Karnani, A., "Generic Competitive Strategies - an Analytical Approach", *Strategic Management Journal*, Vol.5, 1984, pp.367-380; Murray, A.I., "A Contingency View of Porter's Generic Strategies", *Academy of Management Review*, Vol.13, No.3, 1988, pp.390-400; Hill, C.W.L.,

Chapter 4: Michael E. Porter and Sustainable Competitive Advantage

"Differentiation Versus Low Cost or Differentiation and Low Cost: a Contingency Framework", *Academy of Management Review*, Vol.13, No.2, 1988, pp.401-411; Hendry, J., "The Problem with Porter's Generic Strategies", *European Marketing Journal,* Vol.8, No.4, 1990; Cronshaw, M., Davis, E. and Kay, J., "On Being Stuck In The Middle, or Good Food Costs Less at Sainsburys", a working paper, Centre for Business Strategy, London School of Business, 1990; Faulkner, D. and Bowman, C., "Generic Strategies and Congruent Organisational Structures: Some Suggestions", *European Management Journal,* Vol.10, N0.4, 1992.

4. See Linden Brown, *Competitive Marketing Strategy*, Nelson, Melbourne, 1989. See also, McDonald, M. and Gattorna, J., M*arketing Plans: How to Prepare Them, How to Write Them,* Heinemann. London, 1984.

5. See Porter, *Competitive Advantage* (1985).

6. *Ibid.*

Competitive Advantage: Concepts and Cases

WHEN THE GOING GETS TOUGH ...

ASPIRIN WARS

Times are tough and getting tougher in the pharmaceutical industry.

In the U.S., competition is feverish. Earnings are expected to rise by only 4.5% this year while sales, plumped up by acquisitions, rise by only 13%. The glory days when drugmakers could rise their prices at will, reap double-digit earnings gains, and dazzle wall Street are gone.

The balance of power has changed! The relentless price-cutting power of managed health-care buyers is giving the industry a headache.

Now, most of the older, well-established drug companies are in the throes of consolidation. Some are snapping up distributors, others are trying to bulk up product lines or lock in promising research.

Even the newer biotech companies are struggling, many of them reeling from failed products. A 49.9% stake in biotech innovator Chiron Corp has just been purchased by Ciba-Geigy for $2.1 billion, and Synergen Inc. was sold outright to Amgen Inc. for $260 million. Strategic alliances will proliferate as other smaller companies get together to fund research while trying to avoid being taken over.

Perhaps the industry's greatest challenge is to develop new products at a time when, with earnings down, R&D expenditures are being squeezed.

The need to find new products is imperative as more and more patents expire, exposing their former holders to competition from generics. Patents on 17 big-selling drugs - with $8.5 billion in annual sales - have expired in the past two years.

(Adapted from an article by Joseph Weber and Joan O'C. Hamilton, "Take Two Aspirin and Call in the Morning, *Business Week,* January 9, 1995, p.49.)

Chapter 4: Michael E. Porter and Sustainable Competitive Advantage

... THE TOUGH GET GOING

THE BIKER BRIDADE: A NICHE PLAYER IN A BIG MARKET

Two owners of a motorcycle-tour operation are combining their bike and business skills to attract increasing numbers of foreign tourists.

Ron Staines and Alan Peterson are equal part-owners of Australian Motorcycle Adventures (AMA), a company which offers bikers the chance to ride alone or in groups to places as far afield as Ayers Rock, the tip of Cape York and the Birdsville Track.

The company has come a long way since it was started in 1989. It has a small staff and a fleet of 45 motorcycles. The off-road bikes are replaced every 25,000 kilometres and the on-road at 40,000 kilometres.

Almost 90% of its customers are overseas visitors, mainly from Japan. They are typically professional people, aged from 21 to 65. More than 20% are female, and many clients are honeymooners. They hire the bikes from AMA's Brisbane office and are given equipment for the trip, including camping gear.

Staines, the founder, says that it didn't take him long to work out that business skills were more important than biking skills in running the business. Four years ago he brought in Peterson to bolster the finance and administration side of the business.

Staines and Peterson regard it as an "export" business, in that they are earning overseas money. However, to date, they have not been able to convince the Taxation Office to see it that way, and so are ineligible for exporters' concessions. This is despite the fact that they have paid $25,000 to a Japanese advertising agency to promote the business in that country.

The owners see the main risk to their business as coming from other bike enthusiasts who wish to turn their hobby into a business. They say that some newcomers have only lasted six months but that in that time they have done great harm by offering cheap tours that are often poorly organised and poorly serviced.

(Adapted from an article by Murray Massey, "Japan Ad Pays Off For Biker Brigade", *Business Review Weekly,* January 16 1995, p.41.)

CASE STUDY 4:

WOOLWORTHS SIZES UP ITS GREAT COMPETITOR

Woolworths is stepping up the pace of its battle with Coles Myer in the supermarket business, demonstrating its form in recent weeks in tours and briefings to industry analysts whose gaze had switched to its rejuvenated rival.

Woolworths is emphasising its head-down, focused approach to business as the giant Coles Myer comes up fast behind it. The refrain from the Woolworths team is that a consistent operating strategy and a growth-profit record will be their reward.

But the analysts are having a hard time believing that Woolworths can continue to stay so far in front. They think that it may have had its best times and that Coles is poised for a great leap forward after lagging behind for so long.

To convince investors that it is up to the new challenge from Coles, and that it not simply looking over its shoulder at the competition, Woolworths is displaying its plans for new store openings - including its blueprint for "marketplace" style developments - and has put on show its state-of-the-art computer management systems after a four-year revamp.

It has spent $160 million in the first half of the financial year, a high rate of capital spending which reflects its level of commitment to the new store strategy.

The marketplace style developments are the cornerstone of the new store strategy, and will make up about half of the new supermarkets which are being opened by Woolworths. It intends to keep control of these new developments, twenty-four of which are planned. These will be small shopping centres, each combining a Woolies supermarket or Big W store with speciality stores. They will reflect the view of Woolworths that "convenience" will be the byword for the shopper of the future.

The plans are part of what it sees as a growing trend towards convenience shopping at low prices, with the key being customer demand for food shopping. It believes that the fact that most Woolies centres are freestanding or in small centres means more convenience in after hours times, in particular in the early evenings.

In line with this philosophy, Woolworths will continue to grow its successful fresh foods strategy, developing it with delicatessen, in-store bakery, pre-prepared food and pizza.

While price competition remains tight on general merchandise, these new, perishable food products have also given Woolworths a way of lifting profit margins.

It's a fail-safe blend of new store openings, extended trading hours, cost control, and, as a result, pricing power, that Woolworths is arguing will keep it in front.

Chapter 4: Michael E. Porter and Sustainable Competitive Advantage

Woolworths has also spent a lot of effort and resources on computer systems, an area in which it seems to be a step ahead of Coles Myer. During the recent tour of Woolworths stores and facilities, the industry analysts were shown the entirely overhauled computer system which covers stores, distribution centres and corporate head office making it one of the most advanced systems in the industry.

The analysts were told that the computer system will allow Woolworths to cut stock levels by up to $200 million (or about 20%) and also to cut the costs of buying stock in the process. The system is, in reality, a global marketing network on which products can be bought and sold.

The system appears to shore up Woolworths' claim that it has the lowest cost base in the industry, giving it the ability to set prices in the highly competitive supermarket game.

Its costs have been kept tight across all areas, including distribution, promotion and property costs. and analytsts believe that these costs are rising at less rate than that of sales.

The showing-off of all of these store and systems developments seems to be working to prove to investors that Woolworths has the ability to increase profits through continued growth an a superior operating strategy to Coles Myer.

There can be little debate, however, that the competition will be incredibly intense over the next year or two as a major repositioning of Coles and Franklins takes place.

But by any measure Woolworths has a strong case for selling itself as a defensive investment going into a slowdown in the economic cycle with its "slow-and'steady-wins-the-race" approach contrasting with the current scramble at Coles Myer to rebuild its massive business on several fronts before the economy turns against it.

(Adapted from an article by Emiliya Mychasuk, "Woolworths Sizes Up Its Great Competitor", *Sydney Morning Herald*, 20 March 1995, p.24.)

Competitive Advantage: Concepts and Cases

CASE STUDY - QUESTIONS FOR DISCUSSION

1. In terms of Michael Porter's "three generic strategies", what strategy does Woolworths seem to have adopted in its efforts to maintain a competitive advantage? Give your reasons.

2. What do you think is meant by the Woolworths' claim that its computer system is "a global marketing network on which products can be bought and sold"?

3. Do you agree with the Woolworths' claim that "convenience" will be the byword for the shopper in the future? How is the Woolworths strategy catering to the shopper's desire for convenience?

4. What is meant by the assertion that Woolworths' "lowest cost base in the industry" will give it the ability to set prices in the highly competiitve supermarket industry?

5. Explain the claim that Woolworths' emphasis on "new perishable food products" have also given it a way of lifting profit margins? In what respects can these products offer the prospect of higher margins than those in the "general merchandise" category?

6. In what respects can Woolwoths' operating strategy as revealed here be considered as a "slow but-steady-wins-the-race" strategy?

7. Would you agree that Woolworths' "new store openings, extended trading hours, cost control and, as a result, pricing power" is a "fail-safe" combination that will keep it in front? Give reasons.

8. Woolworths argues that "it has the ability to increase profits through continued growth in market share" Is there any evidence available to suggest that a greater market share means higher profits?

9. Of what use would Michael Porter's "industry structure model" be here in assessing the appropriateness of Woolworths' operating strategy? Explain.

10. What would be the effect of Woolworths' costs in all areas "rising at a lesser rate than that of sales"?

CHAPTER 5

The "New Wisdom" of Rosabeth Moss Kanter

As was observed in the opening paragraphs of the previous chapter, the influence of Harvard's Michael E. Porter has been profound in the last fifteen or so years in the areas of competition and competitive strategy. Despite an abundance of critics, it seems likely that his ideas will find ready currency among academics, practising managers and marketers for quite some time to come.[1]

More recently, however, Rosabeth Moss Kanter, another Harvard professor, has pointed to a body of material which could supplant Porter's views in the minds of those charged with defining strategy for their organisations.

New Wisdom

Kanter refers to this material as the "new wisdom" about how to compete.

In 1990, in her (then) role as editor of the prestigious *Harvard Business Review*, Kanter had this to say about what she had been publishing in recent issues:

> *New wisdom about how to compete has emerged in recent years, much of it in the pages of HBR. Such ideas have the potential to shape organizational life by putting social factors at the forefront of business success.*
>
> *Companies are shifting away from defining their strategies in terms of the classic sources of competitive advantage - low cost and differentiated features. In a volatile, intensely competitive world, success comes from the capacity to respond and act - not from characteristics of today's products and markets.*
>
> *Instead, four new bases for sustainable competitive advantage guide the actions of today's successful companies: core competence, time compression, continuous improvement, and relationships.*[2]

Note that in her claim that today's successful company are "shifting away from defining their strategies in terms of the classic sources of competitive advantage - low cost and differentiated features" - Kanter is not saying that *low cost* and *differentiation* are no longer important. These *are* fundamental sources of competitive advantage.

What she *is* saying is that many of today's successful companies see value in *defining* their strategies differently. In focusing on *core competence, time compression, continuous improvement* and *relationships*, they are giving expression to the means by which they will achieve a sustainable competitive advantage through cost reduction and differentiation.

Kanter is quick to point out that the credit for the "new wisdom" belongs to others. In the area of core competence, she refers to the work of Gary Hamel and C.K. Prahalad, Michael Porter, Alfred Chandler and others. In time compression, she acknowledges the work of George Stalk, Thomas Hout and Joseph Bower. In continuous improvement, she acknowledges the special contribution of David Garvin. In relationships, she points to the research of Charles Ferguson.[3]

Core Competence

A company's core competence is a *distinctive skill*, or something it does better than its competitors.

A core competence is often related to a manufacturing process or to some particular application of technology. If an organisation can identify its core competences, it can employ them to advantage throughout its entire operational scope.

In the past, many companies have attempted to achieve their growth targets by diversifying their operations. Spread across a multitude of industries and technologies, their operating divisions have been quite separate entities, often having little in common, and with no particular skill or competence underpinning them.

In the more volatile and competitive decade of the 1990s, however, companies are increasingly basing their growth on a limited number of particular competences which have relevance or application in every part of the organisation. Kanter has used Honda's skill in engine design, Du Pont's skill in fibre making and 3M's skill in adhesives as examples of companies which have based their entire operations around a particular skill.

C.K. Prahalad and Gary Hamel have likened the diversified company which focuses on its core competences to a large tree. The trunk and major limbs of the tree represent the operating divisions. The smaller branches are the operating divisions or strategic business units (SBUs). The leaves, fruit and flowers are the products of the operating divisions. The roots, which nourish, sustain and stabilise the tree are the core competences.[4]

To illustrate, Prahalad and Hamel take the case of Sony, which sees its core competence or distinctive skill as being miniaturisation. This skill is derived both from its high interest in making its products more compact and from its nurturing of the scientists, engineers, technologists and marketers needed to give effect to this. It has required, too, that these groups have a very sound understanding of the needs and wants of its customers.

Prahalad and Hamel believe that a company has to put effort into identifying it core competences. If a company can list thirty or forty distinctive skills, they assert, it has probably included skills that are not distinctive enough to be useful. It is more likely that a company will only be able to identify four or five things that it can really do better than its competitors.

The test of a skill that is truly distinctive is that it: (i) has relevance to all of the company's product-markets, (ii) contributes to the perceived value of the product itself, and (iii) is difficult for competitors to copy.

Chapter 5: The "New Wisdom" of Rosabeth Moss Kanter

The distinction between "core competence", "core products" and "end products" must also be carefully understood. *Core products* are the embodiment of core competences; *end products* are the applications to which the core products can be put.

Thus, if Honda's core competence is "engine design", its core product is "motor engines" and its end products are "motor vehicles", "motorcycles", "lawn-mowers" and whatever other application it produces in which its motors are used. If another company sees its core competence as "kiln management", its core product might be "ceramics" and its end products might be "dinner-ware", "floor and wall tiles", "insulators for use in electrical and electronic appliances", and so on.

To sustain leadership in its core competence area, a company must seek to maximise its market share of core products. This yields the revenue and market feedback that, partly at least, dictates the pace at which its core competences can be expanded and extended. A dominant position in core products also allows the company to shape the evolution of applications and end product-markets.

Prahalad and Hamel deplore what they refer to as "the tyranny of the SBU". They point to the dangers of each SBU of an organisation jealously guarding its own territory, building walls around its own little empire. They urge companies to think of themselves as a portfolio of core competences, core products and businesses rather than as a portfolio of businesses. The company has a potential reservoir of core competences which should be tapped by other divisions.

Prahalad and Hamel believe that the key employees of a business, who are the carriers of the core competences, should be rotated through the company's divisions in a planned program, given cross-border assignments, rewarded for their participation in cross-divisional project teams, and encouraged to trade ideas.

It is interesting to compare the notion of "core competence" with that of "corporate capabilities". Whereas core competences relate to a particular skill at one point in the firm's value chain, corporate capabilities are broader, more general abilities which a firm possesses and which relate to its capabilities across the entire value chain. This concept is discussed at greater length in the next chapter.[5]

Time Compression

The term "time compression" here simply means the ability to do things quicker than competitors.

This covers many aspects of a firm's operations - from the ability to get new products into the market quicker than competitors, to being able to make deliveries quicker than competitors, and to being able to respond to market trends more quickly than competitors.

Kanter illustrates time compression by reference to the ability of Honda to introduce new models more quickly, and to assemble each vehicle more quickly than U.S. manufacturers can. She refers to the ability of Benetton to keep its stores stocked world-wide with its latest fashions and to its ability to beat its competitors in getting every new fashion trend into its stores earlier than its rivals.

In their article, "Fast-Cycle Capability for Competitive Power", Joseph L. Bower and Thomas M. Hout have likened fast-cycle companies to World War II fighter pilots, saying that "they win by pre-empting the opposition's moves". Yet, they assert, being fast is not a new concept in business

Competitive Advantage: Concepts and Cases

strategy. "It has long been a key factor in the success of businesses ranging from Hong Kong's custom tailors to McDonald's".[6]

Today, however, more and more large, complex businesses are sustaining a competitive advantage by making radical changes to the way they manage time. They make faster decisions, develop new products sooner and deliver customer orders in less time. As a result, they add unique value in the markets they serve, and this value translates into faster growth and bigger profits.

Fast-cycle time plays two important roles in today's top companies, according to Bower and Hout. First, it is an "organizational capability" that management builds into its culture and systems. Bottlenecks of all kinds are systematically removed. Second, it is a "management paradigm", a way of thinking about how to organize and lead, and about how to gain an advantage over competitors. In that its message is so simple, it is a powerful organising device.

The studies of Bower and Hout show that companies which develop fast-cycle capabilities achieve better performance across the board:

- their costs drop because production materials and information collect less overhead and do not accumulate as work-in-progress.

- customer service improves because the lead time from receipt of customer order to shipment of finished goods diminishes.

- quality is higher because it is not possible to speed up the production cycle unless things are done right the first time.

- innovation is enhanced because faster new-product development keeps the company in more constant touch with customers who are expressing needs and wants.

Developing a fast-cycle capability, however, is not easy. It requires fundamental thinking about how a company's goods and services are delivered to customers. It means that all parts of the organisation have to work together - often in new and different ways. Bower and Hout make the point that these requirements are not so difficult for small firms but that they present very real difficulties for larger companies where "the system-like nature of the organisation often gets hidden".

Larger companies, therefore, have to work harder to achieve a fast-cycle capability. They must heighten everyone's awareness of how and where time is spent. They must make the flow of operations from start to finish "visible" and "comprehensible". They must highlight the main functional interfaces and show how they affect the flow of work. They must make everyone aware of how the policies and procedures in one part of the company influence the flow of work in others. They must compensate employees for attaining the required capabilities. Most importantly, they must continually reinforce the fact that the firm is a "system" dedicated to the achievement of a fast-cycle advantage.[5]

Bower and Hout illustrate these requirements with reference to Toyota, "a classic fast-cycle company". Toyota's management exemplifies the mind-set that sees the company as an integrated system for delivering value to customers:

- it organises work in multifunctional teams; made up of people from different parts of the organisation, these teams are small, self-managing and dedicated to keeping the actual product and its essential delivery system clearly visible and foremost in everyone's mind.

Chapter 5: The "New Wisdom" of Rosabeth Moss Kanter

- it tracks cycle times throughout the organisation; managers track the output of each stage of production; they make continuing efforts to reduce each activity's characteristic cycle time and therefore the time of the entire cycle.

- it builds learning loops into the organisation; because customer preferences, products and competitors change so rapidly, managers receive accurate data at every level of input; they emphasise on-line learning to keep abreast of market changes.

- it examines cycle times and raises standards; managers continually benchmark against competitors, not only on time, but also on cost, quality and rate of innovation.

- it sets up unusual organisation mechanisms to focus on cycle-time; for example, temporary teams are formed to study the factors that are slowing down operations; they pursue conflict wherever it is occurring; they are encouraged to keep asking "why" until they get to the root of a problem.

- it develops information systems to track value-adding activities; managers try to distinguish the main value-adding activities and to concentrate on these; they are urged to seek out and get rid of the "departmental neuroses" that have deformed the process over the years.

- it makes time count in managing employees; all individuals are evaluated on their contribution to the working team of which they are a part; the idea of "specialists" is rejected (except where they are absolutely necessary) as they often have trouble accommodating new contexts; each individual is asked to have a plan for the positive changes they intend to make.

- it positions people to accelerate their learning; managers and key people are rotated through all of the various operational functions to widen their understanding of the part each plays; meeting time is devoted to the effect of cycle time on competitive position.

The mind-set which practices such as these exemplify differs markedly from that of previous eras, Bower and Hout suggest. Until relatively recently, good management practice stressed that efficiency depended upon fixed objectives, clear lines of organisation, measures reduced to profit, and as few changes to the basic arrangements as possible. But, say the authors, that was the logic of the mass-production machine, and that logic has been superseded. Today's conditions call not for mass-production but for speed of innovation, and that requires new organisational forms and management practices.

Continuous Improvement

Kanter uses the term "continuous improvement" to mean the continual upgrading of all products and processes as the firm strives to deliver a level of quality that is perceived by customers to be superior to that of its competitors in everything it does.

An aspect of total quality management, continuous improvement (or step-by-step upgrading, often referred to by the Japanese term *kaizen*) becomes a central goal in the activities of firms committed to it. They see that the measurement of quality, the obtaining of feedback from internal and external sources and learning are imperatives in their ability to compete.

Competitive Advantage: Concepts and Cases

Kanter illustrates this base for a sustainable competitive advantage by reference to the fact that, by 1990, PepsiCo had overtaken McDonald's in the U.S. as the fastest-growing fast-food operator by continually improving every product and system and every aspect of its organizational structure.

In stressing the importance of continuous improvement, Kanter points especially to the work of Harvard's David Garvin.

In "Competing on the Eight Dimensions of Quality" (*Harvard Business Review*, November-December 1987, Garvin had claimed that, to this time, most U.S. firms had adopted quality practices that were narrow in scope and which were designed merely as "defensive" measures to preempt failures or to eliminate defects. He urged managers to adopt a more aggressive strategy, one which used quality in a "positive" manner as the means to a competitive edge. To make quality gains, managers needed a new way of thinking. High quality, he believed, meant pleasing customers, not just protecting them from annoyances.[7]

He proposed eight categories or "critical dimensions" that could serve as a management framework for the strategic analysis of quality: *performance, features, reliability, conformance, durability, serviceability, aesthetics* and *perceived quality*.

Performance refers to a product's operating characteristics. In the case of tangible goods such as cars and television sets, it means how well the product works (for cars, such factors as acceleration, road handling, steering, braking and comfort; for television sets, such factors as picture quality, colour and the ability to pick up distant stations). In the case of services, or intangible products, it often means promptness of service. While some of these performance factors can be subjective, customer preferences in these variables are so close to universal that they have the force of objective standards.

Features, says Garvin, are the "bells and whistles" that customers expect to receive with the products they buy. Much the same thing can be said about them as about performance standards: while there *can* be subjectivity in what features are necessary, there are almost universal preferences about the features that are expected. However, what is probably much more important in customer choice is not the total number of features built into a product but the *availability* of feature options.

Reliability refers to the probability of a product malfunctioning. Good managers have measures of such reliability factors of their products as the average time to first failure, the average time between failures, and the average failure rate per unit. The unreliability of a product means costly "downtime" for purchasers.

Conformance is the degree to which a product's design and operating characteristics meet established criteria. In the case of tangible goods, the failure of manufacturers to meet established conformance criteria will lead to purchasers having problems with servicing, parts and repairs. In service businesses, a lack of conformance will lead to processing errors, unanticipated delays and frequent errors of other kinds.

Durability is the measure of a product's life or the amount of use a purchaser gets from the product before it deteriorates to an extent that replacement is preferred to repair. Durability has both an economic and a technical dimension. From the technical point of view, durability can often be enhanced by the inclusion of superior materials or by technological improvements in the production processes. From the economic point of view, however, durability standards can vary greatly - not only between different brands of the same product category, but for the total product category over time. For example, the expected life of the automobile rose during the last decade as rising petrol prices and a recessed economy reduced the average number of kilometres driven per year.

Serviceability refers to the speed, courtesy, competence and ease of repair of a product. It includes such things as the timeliness with which service appointments are kept, the nature of the dealings with the service personnel, and the frequency with which service calls or repairs fail to fix the fault or to rectify outstanding problems. Again, much of this is a matter of subjectivity on the part of the purchaser, but in many cases a firm's responsiveness can be measured objectively.

Aesthetics is also a subjective issue. How a product looks, feels, sounds, tastes or smells is often a very personal matter. Nevertheless, there do appear to be some patterns of consumer preferences as shown in ranking studies of these elements of product aesthetics, and firms have to take them into account, even if they knowingly adopt a niche position within the category.

Perceived quality is also a subjective issue; consumers do not always have the information to make proper judgements about the relative quality of the offerings of competitors. Hence, images, advertising and brand building are critical issues. A firm's reputation, says Garvin, is "the primary stuff of perceived quality".

Garvin concludes his article with a warning about what he calls the "shoddy market research" which leads to a neglect of quality dimensions which are critical to consumers. The use of outdated surveys and the assumption that old quality measures are still relevant will lead a company to overlook the competitive opportunities that good strategic use of quality management can create.

Relationships

Here, Kanter uses the term "relationships" to cover a wide variety of alliances and collaborative arrangements that firms, both large ands small, are turning to in increasing numbers as they strive to improve their ability to compete.

Kanter refers specifically to an article by Charles Ferguson, "Computers and the Coming of the U.S. *keiretsu*", (*Harvard Business Review*, July-August, 1990) who argues that if U.S. manufacturers - in every industry, but especially in the highly competitive computer industry - are to compete successfully with their Japanese counterparts, they will need to learn to work together more cooperatively.[8]

Ferguson attributes much of the success of the Japanese manufacturers to the *keiretsu*, the complex web of organisations of many kinds that underpins big business activity in Japan. Linked formally and informally by custom and tradition, religion, equity ownership and social and/or family ties, these *keiretsu* are powerful networks of banks and other financial institutions, manufacturers, suppliers and distributors which work in harmony for the good of all and for the prosperity of the nation.

Such power, says Ferguson, cannot be matched by even the largest and best-resourced U.S. firms acting independently. He warns U.S. computer industry manufacturers that unless they can compete with the Japanese *keiretsu*, the "invented here, made elsewhere" trend which has worried U.S. business since the Second World War is sure to continue. He welcomes the growing trend towards collaboration among U.S. computer firms that he sees beginning to emerge.

In an earlier article, "Becoming PALS: Pooling, Allying, and Linking Across Companies" (*Executive*, Vol.3, No.3, Academy of Management, 1989), Kanter herself explains that "self-reliance", once the catch-cry of the successful U.S. firm, is a thing of the past:

> In the face of heightened competitive pressures and the worldwide scope of both technology and markets, many U.S. firms have established new cooperative agreements with other organisations at home and abroad that involve unprecedented levels (for them) of sharing and commitment.[9]

While American firms, particularly the smaller ones, have always allied with each other for specific purposes, she observes, the extent as well as the diversity of such activity has grown in recent years. It is, in fact, moving from the periphery to the centre of their strategies.

Today, indeed, even the larger firms, those which are in strong positions, more experienced internationally, and in more strategically-important industries, are building their competitive strength through alliances and partnerships.

In doing this, they certainly stand to lose some autonomy (in that they will be sharing certain decisions with their partners) but they do not to lose their legal identity, they retain their own culture and management structure, and they can still pursue their own strategies.

Nevertheless, Kanter warns, the fragility of some kinds of partnerships is as striking as their growing frequency and extent. Studies conducted by McKinsey & Company and Coopers & Lybrand show that perhaps 70% of joint ventures and strategic alliances are abandoned or fall short of expectations. Sometimes, of course, abandonment does not mean failure; it could signify that the objective has been successfully completed. But, there is little doubt that these partnerships are hard to manage.

So, why do they do it? The answer is that such cooperative arrangements have many advantages; they are faster, they are less costly, they are more flexible than "do-it-yourself" options.

Kanter distinguishes three main categories of alliances: service alliances, opportunistic alliances, and stakeholder alliances.

Service alliances are those in which organisations with a common need will group together to create a new entity to fill that need for all of them - an industry research consortium, for example. These alliances are common where the service is too expensive or difficult for one organisation to provide for itself. For instance, in the U.S., The Center for Advanced Television Studies at MIT is a research consortium established by ten independent TV broadcasters to improve the quality of television transmission. It has a yearly annual budget of $1 million.

Opportunistic alliances are those in which individual organisations involve themselves when they see the chance to gain an immediate, although often temporary, competitive advantage. This advantage might relate to the chance to extend an old business or to get into a new market. Usually, this category involves the formation of a joint venture company. For example, in the U.S., Digital Equipment Corporation formed a joint venture company with Allen-Bradley, an industrial controls company, to strengthen its hold on the automation manufacturing market.

Stakeholder alliances are those formed between a number of "complementary" stakeholders in a business process who are involved in different stages of the value-creation chain; they include alliances between manufacturers and their suppliers, distributors and employees. For example, a clothing manufacturer might form a strong partnership alliances with particular suppliers, particular retailers and with the labour unions which represent its employees.

The Importance of Social Factors

In stressing the importance of core competence, time compression, continuous and relationships as bases for sustainable competitive advantage, Kanter, an organisational behaviourist, is quick to observe that the barriers to effective implementation of this "new wisdom" are *social* rather than *strategic*.

She believes that the hardest part of putting them into to practice is the breaking down of the rigid hierarchical structures which still exist in many modern organisations and which inhibit the sort of changes that these strategies require, and the empowering of the people in the organisations who must carry them out.

Nevertheless, she thinks, as continuing to compete successfully in the "volatile and intensely competitive world" of today, and, more especially, in the uncertain world of the future, is coming to depend more and more on the ability to bring the social and the strategic together, the effort that companies will make to do it is not only worthwhile but obligatory.

Endnotes

1. See, for instance, J. Hendry, "The Problems With Porter's Generic Strategies", *European Marketing Journal*, Vol.8, No.4, 1990. See also, David Faulkner and Bowman, C., "Generic Strategies and Congruent Structures: Some Suggestions", *European Management Journal*, Vol.10, No.4, 1992.

2. See Kanter's editorial piece, "How to Compete", *Harvard Business Review*, July-August 1990, pp.7-8.

3. See especially C K. Prahalad and Gary Hamel, "The Core Competence of the Corporation", *Harvard Business Review*, May-June, 1990, pp.79-91; J. Bower and T. Hout, "Fast-Cycle Capability for Competitive Power", *Harvard Business Review*, November-December 1988, pp.110-118; G. Stalk, "Time - The Next Source of Competitive Advantage", *Quality Progress*, Vol.22, No.6, June 1989; D. Garvin's "Competing on the Eight Dimensions of Quality", *Harvard Business Review*, November-December, 1987, pp.101-109; C. Ferguson, "Computers and the Coming of the U.S. 'keiretsu'", *Harvard Business Review*, July-August 1990, pp.55-70.

4. C K. Prahalad and Gary Hamel, "The Core Competence of the Corporation" *(Harvard Business Review,* May-June, 1990, pp.79-91). [This section on core competence is largely based on this article.]

5. George Stalk, Evans, P. and Shulman, L.E., "Competing on Capabilities: The New Rules of Corporate Strategy", *Harvard Business Review*, March-April 1992, pp.57-69.

6. See Joseph L. Bower and Hout, T.M., "Fast-Cycle Capability for Competitive Power", *Harvard Business Review,* November-December 1988, pp.110-118.

7. See D. Garvin "Competing on the Eight Dimensions of Quality", *Harvard Business Review,* November-December, 1987, pp.101-109.

8. See Charles Ferguson, "Computers and the Coming of the U.S. 'keiretsu'", *Harvard Business Review,* July-August 1990, pp.55-70.

9. Rosabeth Moss Kanter, "Becoming PALS: Pooling, Allying and Linking Aross Companies", Executive, Vol.3, No.3, Academy Of Management, 1989, pp.183-193.

Chapter 5: The "New Wisdom" of Rosabeth Moss Kanter

WHEN THE GOING GETS TOUGH ...

PETROL WARS

Caltex chairman Barry Murphy would dearly love to be able to announce at his company's annual general meeting this week that the planned $2.37 billion merger with its competitor Ampol had finally been given the blessing of the Trade Practices Commission.

Although the TPC's approval might yet come in time, it is more likely that it will arrive later. The TPC chairman, Allan Fels, is determined to keep the merger on ice until he is satisfied beyond doubt that it will not reduce competition in the $22 billion industry. It will make the group a very powerful market leader with a 28% market share, reducing the number of major players in the industry from five to four. Using the new section 87B of the Trade Practices Act, Fels wants to extract legally enforceable undertakings from the merger parties to keep competition alive.

The TPC seems to have taken the view that the only real source of competition in the industry comes from the scattered independent retailers. That none of the other three majors - Shell, BP and Mobil - have raised even the slightest whimper of objection to the merger of Caltex and Ampol suggests that the TPC could be right.

Fels may believe that he can use the leverage of the strong desire of Caltex and Ampol to achieve synergistic benefits in merging to enlist the independents to create a fifth force to rival the majors. While this fifth force is unlikely to emerge immediately, Fels appears to be pushing Ampol and Caltex into a position where the partners will provide the means for some of the smaller independents either to merge or to get bigger so that they can challenge the majors on a wider front.

What could transform the scattered independents into a more sizeable foe for the majors is ownership of one or more of the seven seaboard terminals and the fifty retail sites Ampol and Caltex say they will sell or close in the merger rationalisation. While the partners say they have not yet sought buyers of their excess facilities, and that they have no idea what the market for them might be, the TPC is in no doubt that the independents are potential buyers.

But Fels won't be satisfied with simple proposals to sell terminals and retail sites. He wants to know who they are going to and how this would neutralise what he sees as the anti-competitive effect of the merger.

(Adapted from an article by Mark Westfield, "Fels Wants Tough Oil Pledges", *Australian,* 27 March 1995, p.33.)

Competitive Advantage: Concepts and Cases

... THE TOUGH GET GOING

WHITEGOODS WARS

It is not often that a company enters a foreign market and quickly snares up 50% of the market in several mature categories.

But that is what the aggressive New Zealand-based whitegoods producer has achieved in Australia in five years.

Although not taken seriously by Australia's key whitegoods players Email and Southcorp - which between them now control leading brands such as Hoover, Admiral, Kelvinator, Simpson, Westinghouse and Frigidaire - Fisher & Paykel turned the market on its head with an early strategy of high quality products, providing superior service in the retail trade relations and support, and investing substantially in marketing activities.

According to their sales and marketing director, Mike Goadby, Fisher & Paykel now accounts for about 20% of total whitegoods retail sales in Australia, with individual shares in a number of product categories well above that.

In the household refrigerator market (about $350 million annually), Fisher & Paykel recently displaced Email's Kelvinator range for the number two position, and now claims a 20% share, ahead of Kelvinator on 18% and behind Westinghouse on 33 %.

In chest freezers, Fisher & Paykel is engaged in a fierce battle for leadership with Kelvinator. Sales are about even.

The company also has products in the laundry, dishwashing, dryer and vertical freezer segments, with shares ranging from 12% in dishwashers to 28% in washing machines.

Fisher & Paykel has grown at 40% to 50% every year, much of its success being at the expense of key rivals. "Before we arrived, the market was dying for someone to get back to old fashioned marketing and service values. Some of the big organisations had become a little removed from the marketplace," says Goadby.

Goadby concedes that Email and Southcorp are now taking Fisher & Paykel more seriously, and are countering with more aggressive tactics. "But," he says, "in those early years when they thought we were fly-by-nighters, we were out there making growth - and we are not going to give up very easily."

(Adapted from an article by Paul McIntyre, "Fisher & Paykel Reel in the Whitegoods Sector", *Australian Financial Review*, 14 March 1995, p. 6.)

Chapter 5: The "New Wisdom" of Rosabeth Moss Kanter

CASE STUDY 5:

SPOTLIGHT'S COMPETITIVE EDGE

How does a retailer get a competitive edge?

According to the joint managing director of one of Australia's leading retail chains the answer is to scrap traditional management hierarchies and adopt a more customer-oriented and staff-oriented approach.

Mr Morry Fraid of Spotlight Stores Pty Ltd (which employs 1800 people in 56 stores and has an annual turnover of $200 million) thinks that an "empowerment strategy", first embraced by Spotlight in 1986, is what helped the chain to record substantial growth during the recession of the late 1980s and early 1990s.

He describes empowerment as a way of building the competence and commitment of staff. "We want to have the best, most highly motivated people in our organisation - that's been the key to our success," he said. The strategy included the introduction of internal franchising in stores, with profit sharing among staff, and the throwing out of the company's hefty procedures manual.

Fraid says that Spotlight, Australia's leading textile retailer, has undergone major strategic changes since opening its first family-operated store in the Melbourne suburb of Malvern in 1973. By 1983 the business had expanded to eight stores with close to 200 employees.

In a bid to keep up with the growth, the company employed a general manager and established a conventional management structure. The basic purpose of this was "control". The idea, then, was for the managing director at the top to control all the ideas and everything that happened in the organisation. But Fraid's own experience tells him that in that type of organisational structure the people who have the day-to-day contact with the customers are often overlooked. They have the least power to bring about change.

Today, he believes, the conventional structure is inappropriate, especially in service-based businesses, because staff focus more on satisfying the needs of upper management than they do on satisfying customers. "That kind of structure was really working against us at Spotlight," he says. "Staff turnover was high and we were getting more and more customer complaints."

In 1986, Spotlight took the radical step of changing its business structure, placing customers at the top of its corporate ladder, closely followed by the "frontline" staff (those who actually meet the customers on a daily basis). At that time, the company introduced, and still promotes, a "Talk Back to the Boss" policy, which encourages staff to talk freely about their work to their bosses and to suggest ways to improve the business.

Competitive Advantage: Concepts and Cases

To prove it was serious about empowering staff, the company abolished time-clocks for all workers, discontinued preferential parking arrangements for managers, and ensured that staff at all levels received the latest company information and financial statements. A standard in-house discount was introduced for all staff.

Staff were asked to follow one main rule: "Use your own best judgement at all times." People on the shop floor were authorised to make exchanges; no longer did they have to check with the managers before they issued a refund or credit.

For empowerment is to succeed, Fraid contends, it is necessary to have a basic belief that people generally want to do the best job they are capable of, and that they are inherently capable and competent.

However, he warns, there are dangers along the road to empowerment.

"Empowerment without direction is anarchy," he thinks. "Your company must have a very clear vision of where it wants to be, and of how it can get there."

He also admitted that the overhaul in Spotlight's management structure did lead to the departure of some staff. "There were people who willing to change and others who were not," he says. "If you are trying to implement a cultural change in an established organisational hierarchy, there will be some casualties along the way. But, in the long run, you will be better off without these people."

(Adapted from an article by Sue Hobbs, "Empowerment: The Key to Success", *Business Victoria*, March 1995, p.7.)

Chapter 5: The "New Wisdom" of Rosabeth Moss Kanter

CASE STUDY - QUESTIONS FOR DISCUSSION

1. Mr Fraid gives some examples of "empowerment" in his organisation. In what other ways might an empowerment strategy find expression in a retail chain of this kind?

2. Are "conventional" management structures inherently bad or inappropriate, in your opinion? What, if any, are their advantages? Will all companies which employ an "empowerment strategy" succeed in getting a competitive edge, even if the warnings given by Fraid are heeded?

3. Why, do you think, Fraid feels that an empowerment strategy is particularly appropriate in a "service-based" business?

4. What do you think Fraid means by the expression "empowerment without direction is anarchy"?

5. How may a company obtain "a very clear vision of where it wants to be"? Whose vision is it? Is it the vision of all the empowered staff, or of management? Does empowerment extend to the creation of the "vision"?

6. If you were a staff member of Spotlight (one who had to leave the store frequently to visit suppliers or customers), would you object to a non-preferential parking system? (Suppose your store was in a busy area where parking was limited. Would it seem right to you that you had to spend time finding a place to park when those who did not have to leave the store during the day had use of the most convenient parking sites?)

7. Of what use or advantage is it to give staff, as Spotlight's management has done, access to "the latest company information and financial statements? Might there be dangers in this practice? Explain.

8. In your experience, do people "generally want to do the best job they are capable of"?

9. What do you think is meant by the phrase "internal franchising" in this context?

10. Spotlight is not the only business to draw its organisational structure chart with "customers" on the top of the hierarchy. Do you think that this serves a useful purpose or not? Explain.

Competitive Advantage: Concepts and Cases

CHAPTER 6

The Battlefield of the Marketplace: Specific Weapons of War

In previous chapters we have looked at various ways in which organisations attempt to develop, maintain and improve their ability to compete, defining the source of competitive advantage both in terms of characteristics of products and markets and in the ability to respond and act to the challenges of competitors.

In this chapter, we look more closely at specific ways in which competitors go about their quest for an "edge". Passing mention has already been made of some of them; others have not yet been discussed. All deserve our fuller attention.

War in the Marketplace

Likening the battle for marketplace success to actual armed conflict, Kotler, Chandler, Brown and Adam (in their book *Marketing in Australia and New Zealand,* 1994), discuss a range of weapons that are now available to competitors. They put it this way:

> *Just as in war time, the competitors [in a market] search for new ways of breaking through the resistance of their rivals.*
>
> *In World War 1 it was the tanks that could crash over trenches.*
>
> *In World War II it was the atomic bomb.*
>
> *What will it be in the corporate competition of the 1990s?*[1]

Implied in their final question is the notion that the relevance of particular weapons changes over time. Those which are powerful today may not be powerful (or useful at all) in the future.

Some Weapons of War

The authors include in their discussion a number of "weapons" which they have identified as emerging bases of competition: *corporate capabilities; flexible manufacturing; cost flexibility; information technology; total quality management; superior customer service; benchmarking; strategic alliances; and innovation.*

Each of these has been adequately described by the authors. A brief summary of them, however, is appropriate here to account for their relevance. After that, the list is extended.

Corporate Capabilities

Stalk, Evans and Shulman brought the matter of competing on capabilities to the attention of the business world with publication of an article, "Competing on Capabilities", in the *Harvard Business Review* (March-April, 1992).[2]

They make it clear that "capabilities" are not "core competences".

Core competences, as we have seen in a previous chapter, are distinctive skills. As such, they have applicability only at some specific point along the value chain. They are usually technology-based or production-based skills. They are often "invisible" to those outside the firm. For instance, Honda's core competence is its skill in engine design and manufacture.

Capabilities, on the other hand, relate to the management of the total value chain. In this sense, capabilities are "visible" to customers. The authors believe that Honda's skill with engines is not sufficient to account for its outstanding marketplace success. Its *management of its dealer network* has been exceptional, as has been its ability in *product realisation* (bringing forth products that customers truly value). These are two examples of Honda's exceptional corporate capabilities.

Flexible Manufacturing

One of the many tough challenges facing businesses today is the greater fragmentation of markets, as discussed in Chapter 1.

It is becoming harder and harder to satisfy large sectors of the market with one product offering or one product mix. Market segments are splintering into smaller segments, each with unique needs and wants.

In order to be able to target these smaller segments and to satisfy the needs and wants of customers within them, firms need to be able to minimise the long lead-times and expense associated with set-up costs in manufacturing.

They need to be *flexible*. This calls for such abilities as those required to do quite small production runs, to produce more than one item at a time on an assembly line, and to change production processes frequently, rapidly and inexpensively.

In many firms, flexibility of this kind has been made possible by the use of robots and other computerised machinery.

Cost Flexibility

In essence, cost flexibility means having the ability to reduce fixed costs.

By *outsourcing* many of their manufacturing processes, some firms have been able to lower their total costs. The fixed costs of manufacturing (and the costs of the services associated with them) become variable costs.

Chapter 6: The Battlefield Of The Marketplace: Specific Weapons of War

The value of this can be further appreciated if the idea is linked to that of core competence. If a firm outsources in areas other than those in which its distinctive skill lies, its cost flexibility potential is enhanced.

Information Technology

Information technology, as Michael Porter has pointed out, has the ability both to reduce costs and to enhance differentiation.[3]

Costs are reduced when computers and automated processes are used for repetitive tasks, for instance. These tasks might be clerical or mechanical in nature. Differentiation is enhanced when a manufacturer adds value to products by making technological improvements.

Opportunities to reduce costs and enhance differentiation occur in information technology applications throughout the firm's own value chain. But, they also occur throughout the entire value delivery system. For example, many firms today are taking advantage of electronic data interchange (EDI) which enables them to share the information required to meet the value expectations of customers.

Total Quality Management

Whether *quality* can still be considered a basis for competitive advantage today is debatable. By this, we do not mean that quality is no longer important. On the contrary, the ability to ensure that the product's quality is right is more critical than it has ever been.

But, today, many managers believe that quality has to be a "given". That is, they think that if the quality of the product (whether it be a good or a service) does not stand comparison with that of competitors, the firm cannot hope to compete at all.

Those who base their competitive advantage on TQM empower the people in their organisations to accept or reject their own work based upon predetermined standards. In this way, the firm, uses a process of continuous improvement, working towards zero defects, cutting costly waste in time and materials, and adding value to their offerings by lowering price or increasing utility.

Superior Customer Service

Most managers agree that it is far more costly to find new customers than it is to retain their present ones. And the way most go about retaining present customers is by providing superior service.

To do this, they first identify what it is that customers really value in the goods they offer, in the mix they use to communicate and distribute their offerings, and in the additional services they provide. They then go all out to shape the organisational structures and processes required to deliver the value.

Benchmarking

Benchmarking simply means making comparisons.

In an endeavour to approach "world-best-practice", many firms compare their own performance with that of the very best firms thaty can identify to see how it measures up.

The list of variables within the firm's range of busienss activities which can be benchmarked is virtually endless. However, commonly used variables include:

Marketing:

Advertising expenditure; advertising themes; salesforce size, structure, training, experience, compensaion, calls per day, turnover rate, cross selling activity; brand strategy, market share, new product introductions, pricing; distrubution channels used, intermediaries.

Research and development:

Number of patents held, staff numbers, ratio of R & D expenditure to sales, number of government contracts.

Financials:

Capital investment, profitability, overheads, fixed and variable costs, return on investment, return on assets managed, net worth, equity, cash flow, borrowing capacity, debt.

Plant and facility:
Size, capacity, utilisation, equipment costs.

Management and organisation:

Structure, values, general goals and specific objectives, expected growth, decision-making levels, quality control, controls.

Strategic plans:

Short-term, long-term, core business, distinctive skills, acquisitions, integration level, expansion goals, stability level.

Perhaps the hardest task is to identify a suitable firms as the benchmark. Sometimes, the firm to be benchmarked against is in the same industry (competitive benchmarking); sometimes, the firm to be benchmarked will be in a different industry (industry benchmarking). Many companies prefer industry benchmarking to competitive benchmarking, believing that to benchmark a direct competitor is simply playing "catch-up"; their aim is to surpass all rivals, not simply to equal their performance.

Usually, if the firm is seeking to compete on world markets, it will need to go overseas to find the "best-practice" firm it needs to compare itself against. For example, when the Catering Division of Australia's Quantas Airlines a few years ago decided that it had to lift its performance to best-practice level, it went to the Rotterdam waterfront in Holland (the world's busiest sea-port) in search of a suitable benchmark.

Chapter 6: The Battlefield Of The Marketplace: Specific Weapons of War

With a suitable benchmark identified, the firm must then approach the company knowing what aspects of its own operations it thinks are in need of improvement. It must get the cooperation of its chosen partner, which usually requires the divulging and obtaining of highly sensitive information.

If all goes well, the benchmark is established and the firm sets itself to attain the goal, continually monitoring performance until it does.

In the absence (or unavailability of) suitable benchmarks, some firms engage if *reverse process engineering*, obtaining the products of their most capable rivals and taking them apart in the hope of being able to discover manufacturing or cost-saving methods used by competitors which they too can adopt.

Strategic Alliances

Strategic alliances can take many forms - informal cooperation between firms in the same industry, joint ventures, the mutual taking of equity ownership, and so on. All are formed in the expectation that they will provide a strategic advantage.

They may be established for many different purposes.

For example, some are formed by companies wishing to enter new and unfamiliar markets; they may wish to learn from an ally which has already had experience in there. Some are formed by companies wishing to reduce their research and development costs; they may be unable to fund the R&D projects they are working on, or they may wish to speed up this work. Others are formed to eliminate wasteful competition; in the airline industry, for instance, companies will often share luggage handling, reservations and other ground services to obviate the need for each company to have its own set-up for these.

Many strategic alliance fail: because of misunderstandings, often caused by organisational culture differences; because one partner believes it is giving more than it is getting; because one party no longer needs the help the other was giving it; because one party believes the other party is becoming too strong and that it will eventually become a serious rival.

However, despite the difficulties and the high rate of failure, the reasons for forming such alliances, as we have seen, are compelling. The trend is likely to continue for some time to come.

Innovation

Competing on the basis of innovation means seeking a competitive advantage by the creation of new products, processes, new technologies and so on.

Innovation, in this sense, does not mean "creation" or "invention". The company does not need to make great scientific breakthroughs to be an innovator. What it does need to be able to do is to take quick advantage of scientific or technological discoveries, commercialising them in ways which translate the new discoveries into added-value goods and services for their customers.

The Armoury Extended

The competitive weapons in the business arsenal are many. In addition to the bases of advantage already discussed in this chapter, some practitioners are turning to *logistics management* techniques in their quest for a competitive edge, others to the still-emerging principles of *relationship marketing*. Yet others believe that the ability of their firms to compete effectively depends on the empowerment of their *people,* on the strength of their *brands*, on the use *direct marketing*, on more effective *marketing implementation*, and many more.

In effect, the list is infinite.

In very industry the issues upon which competitive advantage rests and the bases upon which an organisation build an advantage will differ. Moreover, in every industry the issues will change over time and with environmental circumstances, and the relevance of the bases of competitive advantage will become greater or less.

Is there a magic formula by which these issues and bases can be isolated and identified? No, of course there is not.

What is required of all managers is that they be *sensitive to the need* to be continually identifying the issues that are relevant to the success of their businesses and *sensitized to the quest* for the bases upon which an advantage can be built. We live in challenging and changing times.

Logistics Management

Success in today's highly competitive business world rests with management's attention the fundamentals: product quality, customer service, and productivity.

The concern with these basics is increasingly drawing the focus of managers to logistics. They are aware that this traditionally low-profile area of business can provide an essential edge in achieving the major objective.

Generally, it is the ability of a competitor to *consistently* meet customer needs that distinguishes it as "winner", and, to a large extent, the consistency of its performance depends on its logistics handling.

Effective management of the logistics mix involves the making of sound decisions about: *facilities* (the type, size, number and location of warehouses/storage yards and the equipment required to operate them); *inventory* (the levels of raw materials and finished product to be held); *communications* (the flow of information to and from the logistics system); *unitisation* (handling and packaging for shipping); and transport (modes, owned or leased vehicles, etc).

Relationship Marketing

The marketing philosophy stresses the need for a firm to satisfy its *customers* completely. But, often, its success or failure in a market will depend as much on its ability to fulfil the needs of *all of its other constituents* as it will on its ability to please its customers.

Relationship marketing stresses the need for a firm to build strong relationships not only with its customers but also with its suppliers, distributors, intermediaries and key influencers, and staff.

Chapter 6: The Battlefield Of The Marketplace: Specific Weapons of War

The staff relationship is of particular concern to relationship marketers. They see *internal marketing*, the winning of the full cooperation of all employees of the firm, as a critical component of success. Unless the internal activities of a firm are handled well, the marketing plan cannot be implemented effectively.

Competitive Advantage Through People

As we have seen previously, the empowerment of their people is seen by many firms as the key to their competitive success.

The claim has often been made that the traditional "Four Ps" of the marketing mix do no allow for an adequate differentiation of a firm's offer, especially when a service component is crucial. It has been suggested frequently that "People" is the vital "fifth P" of the marketing mix.[4]

Superior customer service depends on all of the people in a firm, from management to production, sharing ideas and responsibilities to ensure satisfactory outcomes of every process.

Brand Building

Strong assets and skills are the basis of a firm's competitive advantage, and strong brands are a rich asset.

In Chapter 4 we discussed the role of brands in building barriers to entry. But, according to David A. Aaker, strong brands contribute to the competitive advantage of a firm in two other ways: they help to reduce the primacy of price, and they accentuate the basis of differentiation.[5]

Here, Aaker is suggesting that in making their purchase decisions customers will consider factors other than price. They will often prefer to buy a brand that they know and trust, even if the price is higher. This allows the firm which owns the brand to achieve greater-than-average profits, and this extra margin can be used in ways that further strengthen the brand and/or the firm's overall competitive position.

Strong brands add value to the firm. They enhance its marketing programs attract new customers and hold existing ones; they enhance brand loyalty giving the firm time to respond to competitors' initiatives; they provide a platform for brand extensions; they provide leverage with distributors.

Strong brands add value to customers. They help them to process, store and interpret information about products; they provide them with greater confidence in their choices; and they increase their use satisfaction (that is, a customer *feels* better wearing a Pierre Cardin tie or Longines watch.)

Direct Marketing

As marketers recognise that the needs and wants of every single customer in a market may be different, their ultimate aim is to deliver the offering to each customer by means of a unique mix. For obvious reasons, this is rarely possible.

Direct marketing can, nevertheless, provide a degree of selectivity that most other promotional tools cannot match. Using vast data bases, firms can compile lists of customers according to variables that will influence their purchase and satisfaction: the left-handed, the chronically-ill, the frequent traveller, the antique collector, the book-lover, the cat lover, the real estate investor, and so on.

Such lists allow the firms which use them to personaliss and customise their offerings; to maintain a continuous relationship with their targeted customers; and to measure their responses to particular and precisely-differentiated offerings.

Business Process Re-engineering

Business process re-engineering (BPR) is a way of revitalising organisations which have lost their competitive edge.

But, according to John Sheldon, a partner at KPMG and a BPR specialist, even some of those who are involved with it do not really understand it. They often have difficulty in distinguishing management principles built on this technique from those built on the principles of Total Quality Management (TQM). The essential difference is that whereas TQM is based on *participation* and *co-operation*, BPR is driven by a chief executive whose aim is to *force* improvements in cost, quality and cycle time.[6]

"TQM is like lighting a thousand candles under a steel plate and gradually warming it up. BPR is like using a blowtorch top burn a whole through the plate," says Sheldon.

BPR's main aim is to identify barriers to performance and areas of resistance to change. It involves the basic reshaping of business structures, processes and information technology. It requires a total reorientation of corporate values and culture.

Although it is probably best used in situations which need *radical* change, such as dramatic loss-making or when a new chief executive wants to change a company's total direction, it may be used in more positive situations - to give a short-term boost to sales, for example.

In essence, TQM focuses on continuous improvement; BPR focuses on breakthrough results. TQM seeks incremental improvement; BPR seeks dramatic improvement. TQM seeks to improve existing products and processes: BPR seeks new products and processes. TQM requires low to moderate investment and involves low to moderate risk; BPR requires high investment and involves high risk. TQM is analytical in method; BPR is creative.

Marketing Implementation

Some firms recognise that a lack of effective marketing plan implementation is the cause of their inability to compete.

In this respect, it is difficult to argue with Philip Kotler when he says that "a brilliant marketing plan counts for nothing if it is not implemented properly".[7]

Chapter 6: The Battlefield Of The Marketplace: Specific Weapons of War

Thomas Bonoma has suggested that effective implementation of marketing plans requires the firm to develop skills in the following areas:

- *diagnosis*: Is the problem in the implementation area at all, or is it really a strategy problem?

- *assessment*: Is the problem at the *marketing function* level, the *marketing program* level or the marketing *policy* level? (At the marketing function level the object is to do better market research, create better advertising, build a more effective sales team, and so on. At the program level, it is to integrate the work of the marketing more effectively with the work of all the other business functions with which it is involved - production, accounting and finance, and so on. The policy level, it is to establish broad guidelines to direct the company's marketing effort.)

- *allocating*: Are the company's resources being allocated to the areas where money, time and effort are most required?

- *monitoring*: Are the company's marketing efforts being well monitored, controlled and evaluated?

- *organising*: Is the company structured appropriately to allow for effective marketing implementation?

- *interacting*: Are the company's marketing managers able to interact effectively, motivating and influencing those key people (internal and external) whose support is required for effective implementation of the marketing plan?[8]

Corporate Restructuring

The root cause of the inability of many companies to compete effectively in today's tough business climate is an inappropriate corporate structure. The use of any of the weapons described above may well be of little avail if the overall structure is inadequate.

The decade of the 1980s can now be seen as one of expansion for many corporations. The mood of the times seemed to suggest that "big was better" and, in many cases, firms appeared willing to expand their scale of operations merely for the sake of it. They were lured by the attraction of additional revenues, and seemed to care little whether the businesses they acquired or invested in were in line with their core competences.

In the 1990s, however, the direction of restructuring has largely changed. Many diversified conglomerates may been taken apart, the intention being to make of them more-focused companies.

From this it can be seen that there are a multitude of forms of corporate restructuring: mergers and acquisitions, divestitures, spin-offs, split-offs, sell-offs, equity carve-outs, leveraged buy-outs, share repurchases, and many more. The privatisation of government instrumentalities is a form of corporate restructuring.

It is probably fair to say that the Australian experience of restructuring has been better than that of many other countries. Here, within anti-monopoly guidelines, there have been large mergers in many industries (oil, advertising, publishing, accounting, for example) which have resulted in the fewer but larger companies, better able to compete in international markets and to serve a global customer base.

Endnotes

1. Philip Kotler, Chandler, P., Brown, L. and Adam, S., *Marketing in Australia and New Zealand*, Prentice Hall of Australia, Sydney, 1994, p.677.

2. See *Harvard Business Review*, March-April 1992, pp.57-69.

3. See Michael E. Porter and Millar, V.E., "How Information Gives You Competitive Advantage", *Harvard Business Review*, Vol.63, No.4, pp.149-160.

4. See, for instance, Jim Vandore, "The Missing 'P' in the Marketing Mix is You", *Marketing*, November 1992, pp.56-57.

5. See David A. Aaker, *Managing Brand Equity*, Free Press, New York, 1990, Chapter 1.

6. Some of Sheldon's views were expressed in a short article, "Fast Approach a Double-Edged Sword", *Australian*, 11 March 1995, p.38.

7. Kotler, P., *Marketing Management: Analysis, Planning, Implementation and Control*, Prentice Hall, Englewood Cliffs, eighth edition, 1994, p.738.

8. See Thomas Bonoma, *The Marketing Edge*, Free Press, New York, 1985.

Chapter 6: The Battlefield Of The Marketplace: Specific Weapons of War

WHEN THE GOING GETS TOUGH ...

RUGBY WARS

According to a spokesperson for Optus Vision, the Pay-TV and telephony joint venture which includes Optus Communications and the U.S.-based Continental Cablevision, "Rupert Murdoch couldn't care less about what happens to rugby league."

"Having bought a number of key rugby league players for a 'super league'," he said, "Murdoch wouldn't care if they never played again. What he is really trying to do is to destroy a powerful sport that presently exists with a competitor."

The Optus Vision spokesperson was announcing his company's move to help fund the Australian Rugby League's defence against Mr Rupert Murdoch's planned Pay-TV super league.

"The Murdoch camp has a wider agenda than building a super league," the spokesperson argued. "The super league concept is aimed at damaging Mr Kerry Packer's Nine Network and Optus Vision which are competing against the Foxtel Pay-TV business which is controlled by Murdoch's News Corp and Telecom."

"It is absolutely Murdoch's objective to neutralise his competitor (Nine and Optus Vision). We won't let him," said the spokesperson.

News Corp has taken Federal Court action aimed at breaking several key league clubs and players out of the Australian Rugby League by claiming that some agreements between the parties are in breach of the Trade Practices Act.

The contest between Mr Murdoch and Mr Packer has raised the prospect of two separate leagues, as well as that of a second-tier clash over "free-to-air" coverage of Rugby League between Nine and the Seven Network, with Seven set for a possible revenue windfall.

Seven, which is 15 per cent owned by News Corp and 10 per cent by Telecom, is an essential cog in the News-Telecom camp's Pay-TV super league calculations. This is because a successful super league will be required by the Broadcasting Services Act to provide substantial free-to-air coverage of rugby league, in tandem with Pay-TV broadcasts, to meet the requirements of the Federal Government's anti-siphoning sports list.

The list was designed to ensure that sporting events of national importance were not exclusively shown on Pay-TV.

(Adapted from an article by Mark Furness, "Optus Kicks In To Kick News Out", *Australian Financial Review,* 3 April 1995, p.3.)

... THE TOUGH GET GOING

A TRANSPORT JUGGERNAUT DRIVES HOME THE BENEFITS OF A REJIG

TNT Ltd, the transport juggernaut, has shown the benefits of a three-year restructuring program with a 112% rise in equity consolidated net profit before abnormals to $54 million for the December half.

The restructuring program was undertaken to rectify the troubles of the company in the early 1990s.

Analysts think that the interim result for this year to June 30 could be around $90 million, despite the less buoyant conditions that are expected in the third quarter.

They believe that the effects of the company's restructuring program will not have been fully felt yet. The annual earnings should reflect them.

The company itself has attributed its better results partly to an improvement in the performance of its subsidiaries - including GD Express Worldwide where TNT's share was a pre-tax loss of $9.75 million (down from $24.62 million in the previous corresponding period) - and partly to improvements in the economies of Europe and Australia. (TNT's chief executive, David Mortimer, has said that he expected GD Express Worldwide to end the year on positive results.)

The improved results were also achieved despite the disposal in the period of the AutoLogistics Group and the Holyman Group and weaker earnings from the Australasian interests including TNT's 50 per cent-owned Ansett Airlines.

Overall, TNT's figures are considered its best for three years and indicated the progress it had made. The results have prompted the company to predict that there are even better times ahead for it yet.

(Adapted from an article by Carolyn Cummins, "TNT Drives Home the Benefits of a Rejig", *Australian*, February 22, 1995.)

CASE STUDY 6:

THE TIMES THEY ARE A-CHANGING

Peter Watson's Melbourne Antique Centre is crowded with customers. It has not been this busy for many years. But Peter Watson is not happy. He is in the throes of closing his store after nearly twenty years in the business. His store is crowded with customers today only because this is the first day of his "closing down" sale.

Shrinking retail, more browsers than connoisseurs, a changing market and an onslaught of what he calls "amateur competitors who do not know what they are doing" has led Watson to this decision. When his sale ends later this month he will walk away from a business that once was very prosperous.

"A place like this antique centre has no relevance any more," he says. "Ten years ago, you could line up large sets of Victorian-era chairs and they would all sell. You can't do that any more. People want specialists and professional advice."

"There's no profit in retail. We are making the same in dollar terms as we made in the '80s, but taking inflation into account we haven't progressed in twenty years."

With the boom in retail now a distant memory, Watson intends to focus on the direction he believes the antique market is moving towards - that of a more specialised and total concept of servicing, where customers' queries, needs and wants can be serviced more personally. More in demand than ever are knowledgeable dealers able to discuss each item's value, history and uniqueness, whether giving advice on real antiques (100 years or more old) or collectables (anything that is younger).

But, to some extent, that is what the antique business has always been about. According to the president of the Antique Dealers Association, John Furphy: , "A shop is just a front to introduce people to the service. The idea is to build up trust between dealer and client so that a longer relationship is created."

In Watson's case, the very size of his shop (which includes about 30 stall-holders in 8000 square feet) meant that it was impossible to maintain the quality of that service.

When Watson's store opened in 1976 it was the first of its type in Melbourne, a concentrated hub of retail activity with various stall-holders, where customers could look for select European and English antiques, safe in the knowledge that "not quite right" pieces were virtually unknown.

"In those days," says Watson, "there were only about 80 dealers competing, and there were enough quality pieces to go around. Now there are more than 500 competitors in the market and just not enough antiques. There's a lot of misrepresentation now."

The changing economy has brought about a change in customers, too. With changed financial circumstances, today's customers are younger, more aware, wanting more options, and wanting more service.

As another dealer put in recently: "Basically, the money has gone into different hands. The antique market has become more international. Dealers today have to put more money out for fewer items. The middle market has disappeared, and pitching at the top end is a difficult thing to do. You have to wait longer for that customer."

Peter Watson feels that the recession was the crucial point when fortunes changed for the antique trade. "It put a big division in the sort of person who will buy antiques. In the old days, most of my customers were in their mid-forties. Many ended up broke after the recession, or they had already finished their redecorating."

"Today's customers are thirty-something. They don't just pick out some interesting piece. They want me to do whole rooms - chairs, tables, paintings - the lot. This is not to say we've taken the place of the interior decorator; we don't pick the drapes, for instance. But the customers want *my* opinion. They ask: 'Do *you* think it's nice?' They want reassurance."

Watson plans to open a new store in Melbourne's antique hub - High Street, Armadale. The new store will not be an amalgam of stall-holders; Watson will fully stock it and run it himself. He plans to hold only four major showings a year to which the public and regular clientele will be invited. He will spend the rest of the time in Europe, sourcing fine antique pieces for his exclusive clients.

"Retailing is not the same any more. And the antique business is not retailing at all. It is creating. You've got to create the environment and activity."

(Adapted from an article by Miranda Tay, "The End of an Antique Regime", *Age*, 11 March 1995, p.13.)

Chapter 6: The Battlefield Of The Marketplace: Specific Weapons of War

CASE STUDY - QUESTIONS FOR DISCUSSION

1. Watson says that many competitors were "amateurs". How do you think these "amateurs" were acting, and what would have been the effect of their actions on Watson's business?

2. There is a movement in the antique market to "a total concept of servicing, where customers' queries, needs and wants can be serviced more personally." Do you think that this is unique to the antique business? Either way, what are the implications for retailers?

3. One dealer thinks that "the idea is to build up trust between dealers and clients so that a longer relationship is created". Do you think that all retailers and all customers want longer relationships with each other? Discuss a situation in which either dealers or customers might merely want a "transaction" (as opposed to a "relationship")?

4. How does this case reflect the "serious challenges" faced by businesses today (see Chapter 1)?

5. The "middle market" of antique buyers has disappeared, and finding the "top end" takes longer. Discuss the way in which the top-end, middle, and low-end of this market might differ in needs and wants, explaining how a firm might best serve the customers it targets.

6. "The money has gone into different hands," says one antique dealer. Is this a change in the market that dealers should (or could) have seen coming? How would *you* go about monitoring such market condition changes?

7. Suppose that you one of the 500 competitors in this business, and that you had been monitoring the changes in the market. What might you have done?

8. Watson believes that retailing is "creating", and that the retailer has "to create the environment and the activity". How might these be created?

9. Discuss the relevance of following bases of competitive advantage with regard to antique retailing: corporate capabilities; flexible manufacturing; cost flexibility; information technology; benchmarking; strategic alliances; innovation.

10. Consider the full list of "weapons" of competitive advantage discussed in this chapter. If you were asked to act as a business adviser to a friend who is about to open an antique shop, to which of them would you direct your friend's attention? Give your reasons.

CHAPTER 7

The Ability to Compete

Determinants of Competitive Success

The matter of how a firm can assess its ability to compete effectively in its markets has been left until this final chapter for a good reason: a manager needs to have an understanding of all of the issues that have been discussed to this point in order to make sound decisions about its competitive strategy.

As Peter Doyle (*Marketing Management and Strategy*, 1994) has pointed out, however, whether or not the firm is a "winner" or a "loser" - regardless of its choice of strategy - will be determined ultimately by five factors:[1]

(i) **The "fit" of its offer to the needs of its customers**

Today's outstanding firms are those which are perceived by customers to have products which precisely meet their needs. If customers do not see a firm's product as having some advantage over those of its competitors - that is, offering superior value - they will not buy it.

Moreover, the firm must be aware that the needs of its customers are being shaped continuously by a dynamic environment: changes in the economic, demographic, technological, regulatory, social and cultural and natural environments affect the needs and wants of customers and alter their perceptions of value.

(ii) **Timing**

Paradoxically, the more successful a firm is today, the more vulnerable it can be tomorrow. A firm that adapts its mind-set, assets and skills to meet the needs of today's customers risks becoming irrelevant when those needs change.

To maintain its competitive edge, the firm must be prepared to challenge its own thinking. "Stick-to-the-knitting" and "don't fix it until it's broken" are catch-cries which can become epitaphs.

(iii) **Efficiency versus effectiveness**

Effectiveness is much more important than efficiency to the survival and success of the organisation. Whereas efficiency implies an internal focus, a concern with costs and productivity, effectiveness has an external focus, a concern with satisfying customer needs.

Obviously, successful firms are both effective and efficient, but efficiency is useless if the end result is the production of an offering which has no market appeal.

Competitive Advantage: Concepts and Cases

(iv) Speed and decisiveness

Time has become a competitive weapon. Companies that are fast to innovate, to manufacture, to distribute and to respond can outstrip their competitors and earn better than average profits.

However, speed alone is not enough. A firm needs to be decisive in its commitment of the resources required to sustain the advantage it gains by its speed. Many "first-movers" have been quickly overtaken by competitors which follow them because they have not committed the often substantial resources required to build market acceptance of their products.

(v) Organisational effectiveness

To endure, a firm needs an effective organisational structure. In an increasingly competitive environment, this calls for a structure which allows for the core competences or distinctive skills of the firm - in technology, marketing, distribution or elsewhere - to be utilised throughout the entire scope of its operations. In turn, this calls for a staff which has the commitment to deploy these skills effectively.

Opportunities for Competitive Advantage

Notwithstanding all of this, it is important to realise that the opportunities to gain a competitive advantage can vary in number and size from industry to industry. In some industries there are seemingly endless opportunities to gain an advantage and in others there are few. In some industries the size of these advantages are great, in others they are small.

The Boston Consulting Group has categorised industries - using the number and size of the available opportunities - into four groups: *fragmented, stalemated, volume* and *specialised*.[2]

Fragmented industries are those in which there are many opportunities to gain a competitive advantage - based either on low cost or differentiation - but the size of these advantages are small.

The management of a hairdressing salon, for example, can pursue either a cost leadership or a differentiation strategy very successfully, finding countless ways to give effect to them. But the size of the advantage gained by either strategy is likely to be small. The salon is not likely to be able to make cost savings which are enormously greater than its competitors or to make differentiation enhancements (in service, style, quality, decor, or anything else) which will be so significant as to give it an enormous advantage over its rivals.

In such industries, the pursuit of either low cost or differentiation is unlikely to lead to a significant increase in market share or profitability.

Stalemated industries are those in which there a only a few opportunities to gain a competitive advantage - based either on low cost or differentiation - and the size of them is small.

In some segments of the educational book publishing industry, for example, there are very few opportunities to differentiate the product or to reduce the cost of producing it substantially. To win

Chapter 7: The Ability to Compete

additional business, companies can try hard to hire better salespeople, to entertain prospective clients and the like, but these are relatively small advantages.

In such industries, market share and profitability are likely to be unrelated.

Volume industries are those in which there a only a few opportunities to gain a competitive advantage - based either on low cost or differentiation - but they can be large in size.

For example, a manufacturer of packaging materials (steel and aluminium cans, cardboard, plastics and so on) might have only a limited number of ways to differentiate its product either on cost or features, but it can reap huge rewards and gain a very significant edge on competitors when it is able to do so.

In volume industries such as this, there is likely to be a significant correlation between a company's size and market share and its profitability.

Specialised industries are those in which there are many opportunities to gain a competitive advantage - based either on low cost or differentiation - and they can be large in size.

Manufacturers of precision instruments for use in hospitals and medical research laboratories, for example, have many opportunities for differentiation and cost advantages - and these can result in big rewards.

In specialised industries such as this, market share is not a determinant of profitability and smaller companies can be just as profitable as larger ones.

Assessing Competitive Advantage

Regardless of the type of industry in which they compete, however, all organisations may find it difficult to determine what advantages already distinguish their businesses, how these advantages were gained and how new opportunities for improved competitiveness can be created.

George S. Day and Robin Wensley, in their article, "Assessing Competitive Advantage: A Framework for Diagnosing Competitive Superiority" (1988), have developed a process that can be used to ensure a thorough assessment of the reasons for competitive success or failure.[3]

To begin with, they argue that there is much confusion about the term "competitive advantage".

Some organisations tend to believe that they have a competitive advantage if they have the internal skills and assets which will eventually allow them to out-perform their competitors; in these organisations, the term "competitive advantage" is taken to mean the sources of advantage. Other organisations tend to believe that they have a competitive advantage if their present performance is superior to that of their competitors; in these organisations, the term "competitive advantage" is taken to mean the consequences of actions taken.

Competitive Advantage: Concepts and Cases

Moreover, the authors observe that there are two broad approaches to the way in which companies assess their competitive advantage:

- A **competitor-centered** approach
- A **customer-centered** approach

A *competitor-centered* assessment is based on direct comparisons of targeted rivals. The management of a particular firm focuses on the way in which its offerings compare with those of these competitors. It watches its own costs, matches the marketing initiatives of its rivals, and looks for an edge in technology. In order to detect changes in competitive position in its markets, it monitors all market share movements closely.

This approach is particularly common in stalemated industries where "beat the competition" is usually the name of the game.

The focus of a *customer-centered* assessment is the detailed analysis of customer benefits in all targeted segments and the implementation of the actions necessary to improve performance in them. In this sense it is a "market-back" approach. Relatively little attention is given to the actions of competitors. Instead, customer relationships are paramount and evidence of continuing customer satisfaction and loyalty is more meaningful than market share.

This approach is particularly common in industries where the there is little opportunity to differentiate offerings substantially and where market entry is easy.

Both approaches, according to Day and Wensley, have their advantages and disadvantages. The competitor-centered approach allows for direct comparisons of costs and controllable activities with key rivals but often leads to an obsession with these at the expense of customer needs and wants. The customer-centered approach allows for the monitoring of changing needs and wants within the market but may lead to an lack of management care of competitors' initiatives and controllable activities.

In practice, most businesses lean to one approach or the other, and often the tilt is very pronounced. What is required, the authors believe, is a sound balance between the two.

In an attempt to overcome both the difference in definition of "competitive advantage" and to address the difference in approach to its assessment, Day and Wensley propose a framework for the assessment of competitive advantage that not only distinguishes the *sources* of competitive advantage from their *consequences* but also provides a balance between the competitor-centered and customer-centered approaches.

The authors refer to this framework as the "SPP model": sources, position, performance.

The key elements of the framework or model are:

- identification of *key success factors*
- assessment of *sources of advantage*
- assessment of *positional advantages*

- assessment of *performance outcomes*
- identification of *strategic choices*
- decisions on *relative rate of investment*

The Day and Wensley Framework for Assessing Competitive Advantage

The proposition of the Day and Wensley "SPP" framework is that a firm which has *superior sources of advantage* (superior skills and superior resources) will win a *superior position* (operating at relatively lower costs and/or delivering superior customer value) in its markets, providing, of course, that it makes the right strategic choices and that the quality of its tactics, programs and systems for strategy implementation is high.

A positional advantage will lead in turn to *superior performance outcomes* (greater customer satisfaction and, hence, greater customer loyalty), and the obvious result of greater customer satisfaction and loyalty is more *market share*.

The outcome of a greater market share, as the PIMS Program has revealed, is greater relative *profitability*.

Finally, the greater margin of the more profitable business will influence the *relative rate of investment* back in to the skills and assets to further enhance the sources of advantage - and so the cycle is perpetuated.

The key elements of the model will now be explored in depth.

Identification of Key Success Factors

The Day and Wensley framework first requires managers to identify the *key success factors* for the industry, those operational elements which any competitor will need to "get right" in order compete at all.

These key success factors will vary from industry to industry, from market to market and from segment to segment. The authors illustrate this by reference to the food processing industry, where they list *new product development*, *good distribution* and *effective advertising* as the key factors for success, and to the ice cream market where *the ability to control seasonal variations* and *the ability to ensure economic refrigeration* are also seen to be critical.

Numerous methods have been proposed for the identification of key success factors, but most of these involve the intuitive judgement of industry experts and industry analysts.

Among these methods are:

- the comparison by management of "winning" versus "losing" competitors in an industry in order to discover reasons for the differences in their performance

- the identification of "high leverage phenomena", or the causal relationships between controllable variables (such as plant scale, production run length, salesforce density, and so on) and performance

- the estimation by management of market share elasticities (or the degree to which the total revenues of a company will be increased or decreased by changes in marketing activities such as pricing, sales effort, and service levels)

- the identification of drivers of activities in the value chain (or the examining of each value chain activity to isolate the important strategic relationships between what is done, and at what cost, and the performance outcome)

The authors "regrettably" admit that none of these methods is entirely satisfactory, and that all of them are better at determining *possible* key success factors than they are at isolating those few areas where superior execution or increased investment will have the greatest impact on performance.

Assessment of the Sources of Advantage

Having attempted to identify key success factors, managers who adopt the Day and Wensley framework to assess the competitive advantage of their organisations are next required to assess their *sources of advantage*.

Sources of advantage are seen by the authors to be a combination of *superior skills* and *superior resources*.

Superior skills are the distinctive capabilities of personnel that set them apart from the personnel of competing firms. These are often engineering or technical skills, but they may also be derived from the systems or structure of the organisation, skills which allow it to act more quickly in response to market changes.

Superior resources are more tangible elements for advantage, enabling a firm to exercise its capabilities more readily than competitors. These superior resources may take the form of better locations, larger scale of manufacturing facilities, a larger salesforce, wider distribution coverage, automated assembly lines, better established brand names, and so on.

Assessment of Positional Advantage

The assessment of positional advantage of a business requires managers to consider whether it has an advantage over competitors in terms of being able to deliver *superior customer value* or to operate at *lower relative costs*.

Delivering superior customer value means occupying a differentiated position in the market, or a position in which its customers, perceiving that the firm's offering delivers benefits that are not matched by those of competitors, are prepared to pay a premium price for it.

As we have seen in previous chapters, customers can distinguish superior benefits along a myriad of dimensions: the provision of superior service, a superior brand, innovative features, product quality, more convenient locations, and so on.

Chapter 7: The Ability to Compete

Operating at *lower relative cost* means performing most activities at a lower cost than competitors while preserving parity in the product offering.

The assessment of either positional advantage - delivering superior customer value or operating at relative lower cost - is probably best understood within the framework of Michael Porter's value chain. This, as we have seen, classifies the activities of the business into discrete steps or stages, allowing for the design, production, delivery, marketing and service functions (tied together by firm-wide functions such as procurement, technology, human resource management and the firm's infrastructure) to be examined. Only those activities which have a great impact on customer value or account for a large or growing proportion of the cost need be considered.

Assessment of Performance Outcomes

Having assessed whatever positional advantage the firm may have, management can now turn its attention to the assessment of *performance outcomes*.

The most popular performance outcome measures are *market share* and *profitability*.

The authors assert, however, that the belief that the firm which has the biggest share of the market is the "winner" is a dangerous one. While current market share is a measure of *past* performance, and while the firm which has the biggest market share can reasonably be expected to continue to perform well, it does not *necessarily* indicate that the firm's performance will be superior in the future.

A similar objection is made to the reliance on measures of current *profitability*. Current profitability, too, is a reflection of past performance rather than an indicator of future performance. In this sense, current profitability measures do not provide a complete picture of current positional advantage.

Thus, according to Day and Wensley, the assessment of *customer satisfaction* and *loyalty* should precede the assessment of market share and profitability. These are more sensitive reflections of customer responses to positional advantages.

Competitor-Centered and Customer-Centered Measures of Assessment of Competitive Advantage

As we have seen, Day and Wensley contend that a balanced and accurate assessment of a firm's superiority must, ideally, involve both competitor-centered and customer-centered measures or approaches.

Methods for Assessing Sources of Advantage or Distinctive Competences

Customers can have little to say in the assessment of *sources of advantage* or *distinctive competences* (superior skills and superior resources) because they are not in a position to know how a particular firm has created and sustained superior customer service.

Competitive Advantage: Concepts and Cases

The analyses of competitive superiority in skills and resources are made, therefore, solely by people within the firm using competitors as the standard of comparison. The findings of these analyses do not necessarily tell whether the firm will be distinguished favourably in the eyes of customers.

The methods available for the assessment of sources of advantage are:

Management Judgements of Strengths and Weaknesses

While management judgements of strengths and weaknesses have the virtue of simplicity, they also have limitations. For example, it is often difficult to distinguish what a competitor does well that is important to customers from what it does well that is unimportant to them.

Comparison of Resource Commitments and Capabilities

Comparisons of resource commitments and capabilities have limitations, too. While some "hard" resource commitments and capabilities are readily visible - for instance, size of salesforce, number of dealers and plant capacity - other intangible resource commitments and capabilities - speed of response to service calls, ability to adapt to change, capability to respond quickly to competitors' moves, and so on - might be less visible.

Marketing Skills Audit

While a marketing skills audit sounds like a reasonable approach to the assessment of a firm's own sources of superiority, Day and Wensley believe that it, too, has limitations. Some of the distinctive skills of an organisation may be simply too subtle to measure. For instance, they argue, how can a focus on total customer satisfaction be accurately assessed? How can a focus on continuous innovation be assessed? How can a widespread commitment from all levels of the organisation to total customer satisfaction and continuous innovation be accurately assessed?

In the face of the many limitations of these methods for assessing *superior sources of advantage*, the only recourse is to the knowledge and experience of managers. But here, too, there is often a problem - a lack of objectivity.

Methods for Assessing Positional Advantage

Both competitor-centered and customer-centered methods are available for the assessment of positional advantage.

Competitive Cost and Activity Comparisons

This is a competitor-based method with two approaches: value chain comparisons of relative cost, and cross-sectional analysis of experience curves.

- *Value chain comparisons of relative cost* call for the identification of the value chains of all competitors and for the estimation of the cost of performing the key value activities. Lack of hard data is the chief limitation. While some facts can be obtained by observation, public documents, interviews with suppliers and distributors, reverse engineering and similar methods, some information will always be difficult to obtain.

Chapter 7: The Ability to Compete

- *Cross-sectional analysis of experience curves* involve the comparison of the total cost positions of competitors according to their experience base. With such curves it is possible to estimate the relative profitability of each competitor at the prevailing price. Such comparisons are only possible, however, when all significant competitors are similar in scope, strategy and value chain configuration.

Customer Comparisons of Attributes of Competitors

Customer comparisons of attributes of competitors are customer-based methods of assessing performance. Three approaches are available: choice models, conjoint analysis, and market mapping.

- *Choice models* rely upon customer surveys to determine why they prefer to buy from a particular competitor. Customers are asked to rank the performance of competitors on the attributes that correspond to their purchase criteria. These rankings are then multiplied by the relative importance of the attribute, and totalled, to arrive at an overall customer attitude score.

- *Conjoint analysis* is a statistical technique or procedure which can be used in an attempt to overcome the problem with choice models: that of customer trade-offs among levels of attributes of competitors. (Using choice models, the total scores for any two competitors may be equal and yet the score for each attribute may have varied widely.) Conjoint analysis has the capacity to decompose an "overall preference" or "value for money" score into "part worths" for each level of each attribute.

- *Market mapping* compresses the information about customer judgements about related attributes of competitors into a few composite dimensions. Their main advantage is that they represent pictorially the relationships among competitors from the customers' point of view. For instance, customers might be asked to rate the offerings of competitors' in a segment of the automobile industry along a two dimensional matrix on the dimensions of "stylishness in appearance" (high to low) and "superior performance" (high to low). Such a map might provide a useful insight into the specific reasons why customers prefer one competitor's offering to that of another.

Methods for Assessing Key Success Factors

As is the case with sources of advantage, and for the same reason, customers can have little to say about the assessment of *key success factors*. Again, the only recourse is to the knowledge and experience of managers.

The competitor-centered methods of assessment of key success factors as:

Comparison of Winning vs. Losing Competitors

Identification of High Leverage Phenomena

An explanation of these methods has already been provided in the section on "Identification of Key Success Factors" above.

Methods for Assessing Measures of Performance

Both competitor-based and customer-based methods are available for the assessment of performance.

Customer Satisfaction Surveys

The customer satisfaction survey is a customer-based method of assessing performance.

While the achievement of long-term customer satisfaction is usually high on the list of strategic priorities of firms, few routinely monitor it. And when they do, the information they obtain usually lacks relevance to issues of competitive advantage.

Firms need to measure their overall performance (in service, sales and distribution as well as in product performance) and to compare it to that of competitors.

One impediment to the accurate tracking of customer satisfaction in the past has been a lack of management commitment to the task. Another has been the nature of the survey instrument itself; most surveys have tended to focus on the product or brand most recently purchased and the firm's intentions to repurchase. Seldom are the surveys comparative; nor do they often allow for the isolation of the contribution of each product or service attribute of the firm to the overall satisfaction of the customer.

Loyalty (Customer Franchise)

Measuring *customer loyalty to the brand* (or *customer franchise,* as it is sometimes called) is another customer-centered approach to performance measurement. It requires managers to monitor customer attitudes and biases toward their businesses and products.

Economists have tended to think of brand or firm loyalty in terms of the cost to the customer in searching for a superior offering. That is, they assert that there is brand loyalty when the costs a customer would incur in seeking out a product which offers greater benefits exceed the benefits to be gained by the search.

Although the economist's model may be correct, it is not very revealing. It does not account for the way in which customer perceptions of a brand's worth are formed or changed.

Loyalty is better thought of as a bias toward a particular brand regardless of the price of competing brands or of the cost involved in obtaining them.

Obviously, however, some customers who do have a loyalty bias toward Brand A will buy Brand B if Brand B is heavily enough discounted or promoted. In this case, the brand loyalty is not sufficient to offset the price disadvantage.

Although it is a difficult task, managers must attempt to understand loyalty in this sense, supplementing their measures of customer loyalty with a knowledge of customers' intermediate attitudes when purchasing.

Market Share

The measurement of *market share* is a common method of assessing performance assessment. It may involve both a competitor-centered approach and a customer-centered approach.

- **Competitor-Centered Assessment of Market Share:**

    Most firms track their own *market share* - competitor-centered approach to performance measurement.

    However, market share in a single market may obscure as much as it reveals. For example, if a firm has a 20% share of a market it may be led falsely into thinking its performance is satisfactory. But, if a strong competitor has a 50% share of the same market, the firm's performance may actually be weak.

    For this reason, according to Day and Wensley, firms should also measure their relative share of end-user segments.

- **Relative Share of End-User Segments:**

    Measuring the relative share of end-user segments is a customer-based approach to performance measurement. It examines the variability in relative market share across end-user segments within the same served market.

    A firm's relative share of an end-user segment is obtained by dividing its share in a particular segment by the share of the top three competitors.

    If a firm has the same share in every possible segment, it probably does not have a position that is differentiated either on cost or features. That is, a brand with distinct need-satisfying capabilities cannot be equally competitive across all segments, or, conversely, a business with considerable variability of shares across end-use segments or customer groups is sharply positioned to satisfy a distinct pattern of needs in one or two segments. The assumption on which this is based is that a more sharply focused brand or business can compete more effectively than a less focused one.

Relative Profitability (Return on Sales and Return on Assets)

Relative profitability (or return on sales and return on assets) is a competitor-based measure of performance.

The firm measures its profitability, in terms of its return on its sales revenue and/or its assets, comparing its profits to those of competitors.

Evolving Company Orientations

The argument by Day and Wensley that a company needs to take both a competitor-centered and a customer-centered approach in assessing its ability to compete effectively is echoed by Philip Kotler in his *Marketing Management: Analysis, Planning Implementation and Control* (1994).[4]

He contends, however, that while it is vitally important for a company to watch its competitors closely, it is possible to spend too much time and energy in this activity. A company can become so competitor-centered that it can lose its customer focus. Clearly, a company which is customer-centered is in a better position to identify new opportunities and set a strategy course that will bring it more success in the long-run.

In today's difficult business conditions, Kotler believes, companies must watch both customers and competitors. He sees this as one of four different orientations which have evolved over time: product orientation, customer orientation, competitor orientation and market orientation.

In earlier times, says Kotler, companies tended to pay little attention to either their customers or their competitors. Generally, they were product-oriented.

Later, as the capacity to supply began to outstrip demand in most industry sectors, companies they became customer-oriented. They had come to realise that marketing principles were important, that the key to the achievement of organisational goals was the efficient and effective satisfaction of customer needs and wants.

However, as the competitive environment became increasingly more difficult, they had little choice but to cultivate competitiveness. Many became too competitor-oriented.

Today, excellent companies attempt to balance both of these later orientations. While attempting to remain attuned to the ever-changing needs and wants of their customers, they watch the moves of their competitors closely. They are market-oriented.

Endnotes

1. Peter Doyle, *Marketing Management Strategy*, Prentice Hall International, Hemel Hempstead, 1994, pp.21-23.

2. As quoted by Philp Kotler in *Marketing Management: Analysis, Planning, Implementation and Control,* Prentice Hall, Englewood Cliffs, eighth edition, 1994, p.294.

3. George S. Day and Wensley, R., "Assessing Competitive Advantage: A Framework for Diagnosing Competitive Advantage", *Journal of Marketing*, Vol.52, April 1998, pp.1-20.

4. Philip Kotler, *Marketing Management: Analysis, Planning Implementation and Control*, Prentice Hall, Englewood Cliffs, eighth edition, 1994, p.242.

Chapter 7: The Ability to Compete

WHEN THE GOING GETS TOUGH ...

HOPING FOR A STYLISH SUCCESS

The fashion house, Palmer Corp, is struggling for survival in a very competitive environment.

In a radical bid to halt a drastic decline in revenue, it has appointed an engineer who successfully ran a Sydney computer company as its new general manager.

In another surprise move, Mrs Adele Palmer, the founder of the company, has been re-appointed as creative director. She had been scaling back her involvement in the company during the past two years for personal and internal management reasons.

Mr Eddy Chua, who qualified as an engineer and chartered accountant from Sheffield University in the United Kingdom, has been brought in to increase the turnover by putting logistics and financial systems in place for Palmer Corp.

Malaysian-born Mr Chua, who succeeded in increasing the turnover for the computer company from $1 million to $50 million, will attempt to lift Palmer Corp's figure from $51 million to $70 million over the next three years. After a period of unsettled management and a $5.05 million loss for the half year of this financial year, the company is hoping to be in profit by 1995-96.

At the centre of the company's survival strategy are logistics and design improvements for its "Jag" and "Adele Palmer" labels. "Certainly on the logistics side, I can add value," says Mr Chua.

His appointment is expected to raise eyebrows in the fashion industry, where creative managers are usually appointed to key executive positions.

But Mr Chua believes that there are business similarities between the design and servicing of personal computers and the design of fashion. "They're both very competitive markets," he argues. "You need to come up with new products and new designs all the time. You are in an environment where service and delivery are critical to success."

Connected with this is a need at Palmer Corp to redesign the company's management information systems. These are "not up to the minute", according to Palmer Corp's managing director, Mr John O'Brien.

(Adapted from an article by Lou Caruana, "Eddy's Computer Logic Hits the Catwalk", *Australian*, 31 March, 1995, p.25)

Competitive Advantage: Concepts and Cases

... THE TOUGH GET GOING

OIL AND COAL WARS

Mr Cor Herkstroter, the chairman of Royal Dutch Shell's top-level committee of managing directors, yesterday announced a number of structural changes, saying that these had been triggered by his company's declining performance against its international competitors.

Although the Shell Group had reported net income of four billion pounds sterling (A$8.3 billion), Mr Herkstroter said: "There were too many instances where we were outperformed by our competitors."

However, the restructuring referred to by Mr Herkstroter will mostly by-pass the oil and coal operations of the Australian division of Shell. They may, in fact, lead eventually to the local arm playing a greater role in the Shell Group's operations in Asia.

Shell Australia had already been trimming its own operations and returning to its core interests of oil, gas and coal. In the past year the gold division was sold into a new company, Acacia Resources, and it had sold off its interest in Worsley Alumina joint venture. A concerted effort had also been made to focus on the management skills of the company, with peripheral operations being farmed out to contractors where possible.

This was a significant change in culture for the local operations but the changes, which still have four years to run before Shell can call itself a lean operation producing solid profits, should buffer the company against the forces now shaking its parent.

The proposed restructure at Royal Dutch Shell, an Anglo-Dutch group, will be its biggest shake-up in thirty years. About 1,200 of its 3,900 staff at its offices in The Hague and London will lose their jobs if the changes are made. Among the number of redundancies are some very senior managers. The company believes that it is time to make generational changes.

But the main aims of the plan, devised by the McKinsey consulting group, are the elimination of layers of bureaucracy worldwide, a reduction of the committee culture, and the streamlining of decision-making.

(Adapted from an article by B.G. Yovovich, "'Bad' Ideas Could Be Just What You Need", *Business Marketing*, December 1994, p.22.) Reprinted with permission from the December 1994 issue of *Business Marketing*. Copyright, Crain Communications, Inc.

Chapter 7: The Ability to Compete

CASE STUDY 7:

"BAD" IDEAS THAT WIN AN AGE OF HYPERCOMPETITON

Today, powerful forces are turning the business marketplace upside down. These forces are placing a premium on the firm's ability to recognize and pursue the right kind of "bad idea".

In fact, the time has come to sing the praise of "bad" ideas. Not all bad ideas, mind you, just those that are actually good ideas in disguise.

We've crossed into a new era of "hypercompetitiveness" - one with increased access to management know-how, capital, improved technology, reverse-engineering capabilities, and accelerated responses to competitors' innovations. As a result, traditional business strategies that rely solely on core competences and the incremental building of advantages are likely to relegate a company to a painful and unrewarding business version of trench warfare.

Thus, in this hypercompetitive age, what is really needed is the element of strategic surprise. And, surprising your competitors means successfully pursuing what others consider "bad" ideas.

Dartmouth's business school professor Richard A. D'Aveni, who explored these issues in his recently published book, *Hypercompetition: Managing the Dynamics of Strategic Competition* (Free Press, New York, 1994), thinks that the essence of strategic surprise is doing something that everyone else considers impossible. He says: "Real surprise comes when people say, 'You can't do that' - and you do it. If you tell someone else your idea and they laugh at you and call you an idiot, that's when you know that you can use it to beat them."

There is no set formula for coming up with a "bad" idea. It is not a simple thing to do. Managers and senior executives who have climbed the rungs of the traditional corporate ladder, for example, find it an almost impossible thing to do. After all, their success has been based on coming up with ideas that everyone can see are "good ".

Nevertheless, Professor D'Aveni has described a process that he has been using with companies trying to develop hypercompetitive strategies. It purpose is to increase the likelihood of producing novel ideas.

The process begins with brainstorming. Company representatives from a broad array of functions and managerial perspectives - that go well beyond senior management levels - are assembled, and given the standard instruction to operate in a purely idea-generating mode. No one is allowed to "shoot down" another's idea. This is particularly vital to the generation of breakthrough ideas, warns D'Aveni. "Whenever you find the shoot-down environment, for almost every breakthrough idea, you can find a reason why you don't want to do it."

The group then has a two-pronged mission: to come up with ideas (without the necessity to worry about their real-world feasibility) that would:

(i) dramatically delight current customers and create future customers, and

(ii) excite that other crucial set of stakeholders, the employees.

"You want ideas that motivate the troops to be involved," D'Aveni emphasises. "You need more than just empowerment. You have to ask yourself: 'What are the troops ready to fight for?'"

A dangerous temptation can develop once this first step has been completed and the list of potential strategic thrusts has been compiled. That temptation is to stand back and to see which of the new ideas can best be leveraged off the firm's existing core competences.

That temptation is to be avoided at all costs, thinks D'Aveni. It would make the firm far too predictable. It would be to give up the element of surprise and the opportunity to disrupt the marketplace.

Instead, once the list has been compiled, it should be turned over to the most negative people in your company, whose assignment it should be to tear the ideas to pieces and to make another list - of reasons why these ideas will not work.

The final step is to take both lists to the firm's "can-do" types and to the people who are the high-risk takers. These people are assigned the task of taking the objections of the "negatives" apart, piece by piece, and finding ways around them.

Of course, the process does not *always* produce a a viable strategic thrust. Nor does it *always* yield an idea deemed to be worth attempting. And even when it does yield an idea that is tempting to run with, you cannot expect to get consensus support for it. After all, if you did get consensus support, you could be sure that the idea would be bland, dull and absolutely predictable.

But, if a loud chorus of "It's a bad idea" greets the proposed new idea, that's just fine. You've got them right where you want them.

(Adapted from an article by B.G. Yovovich, "'Bad' Ideas Could Be Just What You Need", *Business Marketing*, December 1994, p.22)

Chapter 7: The Ability to Compete

CASE STUDY - QUESTIONS FOR DISCUSSION

1. Discuss the term "hypercompetition". Explain what Yovovich means when he asserts that we have "crossed into a new age of hypercompetitiveness". Illustrate, with examples, each of the features Yovovich lists as characteristic of this age.

2. Is Professor Richard A. D'Aveni saying that he believes that core competences should be disregarded altogether as a company formulates its competitive strategy? Discuss.

3. What is meant by the notion that the "incremental building of advantages" are likely to relegate a company "to the painful and unrewarding business version of trench warfare." Are Yovovich and D'Aveni saying that this approach is a waste of time?

4. Discuss each stage of D'Aveni's "process" for helping companies to develop hypercompetitive strategies, explaining what is involved, suggesting problems which might occur at each stage and ways to overcome them.

5. What, in practical terms, is meant by the term "empowerment" when considering the way in which staff involvement is sought in developing and implementing strategy. Discuss what D'Aveni means by "you need more than empowerment" to implement his own process. What is that he believes a firm needs?

6. Giving examples, explain the notion of "breakthrough" ideas.

7. Why is the "shoot down" mentality dangerous in brainstorming sessions? Why is it particularly dangerous in brainstorming for breakthrough ideas?

8. Considering Rosabeth Moss Kanter's thought that the barriers to the implementation of her "new wisdom" about how to compete are social rather than strategic, explain the idea of "negatives", "can-do types" and "high-risk takers" in organisations.

9. In view of the fact that customers have to pay for the products they buy from organisations (and that, often, the better the product, the higher the price), is customer "delight" ever really possible?

10. In fact, should a firm even try to "delight" its customers? If a firm really wanted to delight its customers, wouldn't it give its products to its customers free of charge? Isn't a firm's real purpose to delight its shareholders? Are these two objectives contradictory?

Bibliography

Chapter 1: The Quest For Competitive Advantage

Aaker, D.A., *Strategic market management*, John Wiley & Sons, Boston, 1984.

Abell, D.F., *Defining the business: the starting point of strategic planning*, Prentice-Hall, Englewood Cliffs, 1980.

Argenti, J., *Corporate collapse: the causes and symptoms*, McGraw-Hill, London, 1976.

Bain, J.S., *New barriers to competition*, Harvard University Press, Cambridge, MA, 1956.

Bartlett, C. and Ghoshal, S., "Managing across borders: the transnational solution", *Harvard Business School Press*, Boston, 1989.

Bhide, A., "Hustle as strategy", *Harvard Business Review*, September-October 1986.

Boston Consulting Group, *Perspective on experience*, BCG Inc., Boston, 1970.

Caves, R.E. and Porter, M.E., "From entry barriers to mobility barriers: conjectural decisions and contrived deterrence to new competition", *Quarterly Journal of Economics*, 91, 1977.

Cravens, D. and Shipp, S., "Market-driven strategies for competitive advantage", *Business Horizons*, Vol.34, No.1, January/February 1991.

Day, George S, *Strategic marketing planning: the pursuit of competitive advantage*, West Publishing Company, New York, 1984.

Day, G.S., *Analysis for strategic market decisions*, West Publishing Company, New York, 1986.

Day, George S., *Market-driven strategy: processes for creating value*, Free Press, New York, 1990.

Doyle, Peter, *Marketing management strategy*, Prentice Hall International, Hemel Hempstead, 1994.

Drobis, David R., "Competitive thinking for competitive advantage", *Public Relations Quarterly*, Vol.36, No.3, Fall 1991.

Ghemawat, P., "Sustainable advantage", *Harvard Business Review*, September-October, 1986.

Ghemawat, P., *Commitment: the dynamic of strategy*, Free Press, New York, 1991.

Gordon, I., "Shadow your competitors", *World Executive's Digest*, April 1993.

Hamel, Gary and Prahalad, C.K., *Competing for the future,* Harvard Business School Press, Boston, 1994.

Hall, William K., "Survival strategies in a hostile environment", *Harvard Business Review*, 58, Sept-Oct 1980.

Holden, E. and Schiller, Z., "Marketing globally, thinking locally", *Business Week*, May 13, 1991.

Hooley, G. and Saunders, J., *Competitive positioning*, Prentice-Hall International (U.K.), Hemel Hempstead, 1993.

Hout, T., Porter, M.E. and Rudden, E., "How global companies win out", *Harvard Business Review*, September-October, 1982.

James, B., "Reducing the risks of globalisation", *Long Range Planning*, Vol.23, No.1, 1990.

James, D. and Stevens, M., "Changing ground rules force new measures of advantage", *Business Review Weekly*, September 13, 1991.

Kilman, R.H., et al, *Making organisations competitive*, Jossey-Bass, San Francisco, 1991.

Kotler, Philip, *The new competition*, Prentice-Hall, Englewood Cliffs, 1985.

Kotler, Philip, *Marketing management: analysis, planning, implementation and control,* Prentice Hall, Englewood Cliffs, 7th edition 1991; 8th edition 1994.

Kotler, Philip., Chandler, P., Brown, L. and Adam, S., *Marketing in Australia and New Zealand,* Prentice Hall of Australia, Sydney, 3rd edition, 1994.

Legge, John M., *The competitive edge*, Allen and Unwin, Sydney, 1992.

Levitt, T., "The globalisation of markets", *Harvard Business Review*, September-October, 1982.

Levitt, T., *The marketing imagination*, Free Press, New York, revised 1986.

McLaughlin, Peter, "Business and sustainable development", *Business Council Bulletin*, November 1991.

McNamee, Patrick, *Developing strategies for competitive advantage*, Pergamon Press, Oxford, 1991.

Moore, James F., "Predators and prey: a new ecology of competition", *Harvard Business Review*, May-June, 1993.

Moore, John I., *Writers on strategy and strategic management*, Penguin Books, London, 1992.

Oliva, T., Day, D. and DeSarbo, W.S., "Selecting competitive tactics: try a strategy map", *Sloan Management Review*, Spring 1987.

Ohmae, Kenichi, *The borderless world*, Harper Business, New York, 1990.

Ohmae, Kenichi, *Triad power: the coming shape of global competition*, Free Press, 1991.

Porter, M.E., "Changing patterns of international competition", *California Management Review*, Winter 1986.

Porter, Michael, "New global strategies for competitive advantage", *Planning Review*, Vol.18, No.3. May/June 1990.

Porter, Michael E., "From competitive advantage to corporate strategy", *Harvard Business Review*, May-June 1987.

Quelch, J.A. and Hoff, E.J., "Customising global marketing", *Harvard Business Review*, May-June 1986.

Ries, J. and Trout, A., *Marketing Warfare*, McGraw-Hill, New York, 1986.

Ries, J. and Trout, A., *The 22 Immutable Laws of Marketing*, Harper Collins, New York, 1993.

Rothschild, W., *How to gain and maintain a competitive advantage,* McGraw Hill, New York, 1984.

Van den Bosch, F. and Van Prooijen, A., "European management: an emerging competitive advantage of European nations", *European Management Journal*, Vol.10, No.4, December 1992.

Van Gorder, B.E., "Total customer service: the real competitive edge", *Credit*, Vol.16, No.6, Nov/Dec 1990.

Yesawich, P., "The marketplace: value provides competitive edge", *Lodging Hospitality*, Vol.48, No.8, August 1992.

Chapter 2: The Economist's View of Competition

Reynolds, L.G., *Economics: a general introduction*, Irwin, Homewood, Illinois, 4th edition, 1973.

Samuelson, P.A. et al, *Economics*, McGraw-Hill, Sydney, 3rd Australian edition, 1992.

McConnell, C.R. and Brue, S.L., *Economics: principles, problems and policies*, McGraw-Hill, New York, 11th edition, 1990.

Jackson, J. and McConnell, C.R., *Economics*, McGraw-Hill, Sydney, 3rd edition, 1988.

Morgan, E.V., *Economics*, Pitman, London, 1973.

Robinson, J. and Eatwell, J., *An introduction to modern economics*, McGraw-Hill (UK), Maidenhead, 1973.

Howard, W.W. and Dale, E.L., *Contemporary economics: principles and policies*, D.C.Health and Co., Lexington, 1971.

Goodwin, R.M., *Elementary economics from the higher standpoint*, Cambridge University Press, Cambridge, 1970.

Craven, J., *Introduction to economics: an integrated approach to fundamental principles*, Blackwell, London, 1984.

Cauley, T.J., *Economics: principles and institutions*, International Textbook Co., Scranton, PA, 1968.

Dolan, E.G. and Lindsey, D.E., *Economics*, Dryden Press, Chicago, 6th edition, 1991.

Miller, R.J. and Shade, E.D., *Foundations of economics*, Longman Cheshire, Melbourne, 3rd edition, 1990.

Silk, L.S., *Contemporary economics: principles and issues*, McGraw-Hill, New York, 1970.

Hunt, E.K. and Sherman H.J., *Economics: an introduction to traditional and radical views*, Harper & Row, New York, 1972.

Gisser, M. and Barth, P.S., *Basic economics*, International Textbook Co., Scranton, PA, 1970.

Melotte, Y.M. and Moore, R., *Economics*, Prentice-Hall, Englewood Cliffs, 1995.

Challen, D.W. et al, *Principles of economics: income, wealth and welfare in Australia*, Longman Cheshire, Melbourne, 1985.

Elkins, P. and Max-Neef, M. (eds.), *Real-life economics: understanding wealth creation*, Routledge, New York, 1992.

Chapter 3: Competitive Advantage and the Marketing Discipline

Achrol, Ravi S., "Evolution of the marketing organisation: new forms for the turbulent environments", *Journal of Marketing*, October 1991.

Bennett, Rex, "Marketing and competitive advantage: how to satisfy the customer profitably", *Bank Marketing*, Vol.24, No.1, Jan. 1992, pp.36-37.

Bloom, P.N. and Kotler, P., "Strategies for high market share companies", *Harvard Business Review*, Nov-Dec, 1975.

Bonoma, T., *The marketing edge: making strategies work*, Free Press, New York, 1985.

Brock, John J., "Competitor analysis: some practical approaches", *Industrial Marketing Management*, 13, October 1984.

Brown, Linden, *An empirical study and evaluation of marketing strategies adopted in consumer markets*, unpublished PhD thesis, University of New South wales, 1975.

Brown L., *Competitive marketing strategy: developing, maintaining and defending competitive position*, Nelson, Melbourne, 2nd edition, 1995.

Czepiel, John, *Competitive marketing strategy*, Prentice-Hall, Englewood Cliffs, 1992.

Davidson, J.H., *Offensive marketing, or how to make your competitors follow*, Penguin, Harmmondsworth, 1987.

Griffith, M.J., "Marketing strategies for different competitive positions", *Journal of Health Care Marketing*, Vol.9, No.3. September 1989.

Hamermesh, R.G., Anderson, M.J. and Harris, J.E., "Strategies for low-share business", *Harvard Business Review*, May-June, 1978.

Kotler, P., *Marketing management: analysis, planning, implementation and control*, Prentice Hall, Englewood Cliffs, 1994.

Lillis, G. et al, "Marketing strategy to achieve market-share goals", in *Strategic marketing and management*, John Wiley and Sons, Boston, 1985.

McKenna, R, "Marketing is everything", *Harvard Business Review*, September-October, 1992.

Power, C., Konrad, W. and Treece, James B., "Value marketing: quality, service and fair pricing are the keys to selling in the 90s", *Business Week*, 11 November 1991.

Ries, A. and Trout, J., *Positioning: the battle for your mind*, McGraw-Hill, New York, 1986.

Ries, A. and Trout, J., *Marketing warfare*, McGraw-Hill, New York, 1986.

Saunders, J. "Marketing and competitive success", in Baker, M.J., *The marketing book*, Heinemann. London, 1987.

Stern, A.L., "New marketing game: stealing customers", *Dun's Business Month*, February 1985.

Wasson, C.R., *Product management: product life-cycles and competitive marketing strategy*, Challenge Books, Illinois, 1971.

Willigan, G.E., "High-performance marketing: an interview with Nike's Phil Knight", *Harvard Business R*eview, July-August 1992.

Chapter 4: Michael E. Porter and Sustainable Competitive Advantage

Cronshaw, M., Davis, E. and Kay,J., "On being stuck in the middle, or good food costs less at Sainsbury's", Centre for Business Strategy, London School of Business, 1990.

Dess, G.G. and Davis, P.S., "Porter's (1980) generic strategies as determinant's of strategic group membership and organisational performance", *Academy of Management Review,* Vol.27.

Faulkner, D. and Bowman, C., "Generic strategies and congruent organisational structures", *European Management Journal*, Vol.10, No.4, December 1992.

Grant, Robert M., "Porter's *Competitive Advantage of Nations*: an assessment", *Strategic Management Journal*, Vol.12, No.7, Oct.1991.

Hendry, J., "The problem with Porter's generic strategies", *European Marketing Journal*, Vol.8, No.4, 1990.

Hill, C.W., "Differentiation versus low cost or differentiation and low cost: a contingency framework", *Academy of Management Review*, Vol.13, 1988.

Karnani, A., "Generic competitive strategies - an analytical approach:, *Strategic Management Journal,* Vol.7, 1986.

Mathur, S.S., "How firms compete: a new classification of generic strategies", *Journal of General Management* (U.K.), Vol.14, Autumn 1988.

McNamee, P. and McHugh, M., "Competitive strategies in the clothing industry", *Long Range Planning*, Vol.22, No.4, 1989.

Miller, D. and Friesen, P.H., "Porter's (1980) generic strategies and performance: an empirical examination with American data; Part 1: Testing Porter", *Organization Studies*, Vol.7, 1986.

Murray, A.I., "A contingency view of Porter's 'generic strategies'", *Academy of Management Review*, Vol.13, 1988.

Porter, Michael E., "How competitive forces shape strategy", *Harvard Business R*eview, March-April 1979.

Porter, Michael E., *Competitive strategy: techniques for analyzing industries and competitors*, Free Press, New York, 1980.

Porter, Michael E., *Cases in competitive strategy*, Free Press, New York, 1982.

Porter, Michael E., *Competitive advantage: creating and sustaining superior performance*, Free Press, New York, 1985.

Porter, Michael E., *The competitive advantage of nations*, Free Press, New York, 1990.

White, R.E., "Generic business strategies, organisational context and performance: an empirical investigation", *Strategic Management Journal*, Vol.7, 1986.

Wood, Alan, "Economy poised to prove guru of global competition wrong", *Australian*, 8 September 1992.

Wright, P., "A refinement of Porter's strategies", *Strategic Management Journal*, Vol.8, 1987, pp.93-101.

Yetton, P., Craig, J., Davis, J. and Hilmer, F., "Are Diamonds a Country's Best Friend?: A Critique of Porter's Theory of National Competition as Applied to Canada, New Zealand and Australia", *Australian Journal of Management*, September, 1992.

Chapter 5: The "New Wisdom" of Rosabeth Moss Kanter

Anderson, James C. and Narus, James A., "Partnering as focused market strategy", *California Management Review*, Spring 1991.

Bartlett, C. and Ghosal, S., "Managing across borders: the transnational solution", *Harvard Business School Press*, Boston, 1989.

Bleeke, Joel and Ernst, David, "The way to win in cross-border alliances", *Harvard Business Review*, November-December 1991.

Borys, B. and Jemison, D., "Hybrid arrangements as strategic alliance: theoretical issues in organisational combinations", *Academy of Management Review*, Vol.14, 1989.

Bower, Joseph L. and Hout, Thomas M., "Fast-cycle capability for competitive power", *Harvard Business Review*, Vol.66, No.6, November-December, 1988.

Cohen, William A., "War in the marketplace", *Business Horizons*, March-April, 1986.

Ferguson, Charles, "Computers and the Coming of the U.S. '*kieretsu*'", *Harvard Business Review*.

Garvin, David A., "Competing on the eight dimensions of quality", *Harvard Business Review*, Vol.65, No.6, November-December, 1987.

Garvin, David A., "Quality problems, policies, and attitudes in the United States and Japan: an exploratory study", *Academy of Management Journal*, Vol.29, No.4, (Dec. 1986).

Gronhaug, K. and Nordhaug, O., "Strategy and competence in firms", *European Management Journal*, Vol.10, No.4, December 1992.

Gugler, Philippe, "Building transnational alliances to create competitive advantage", *Long Range Planning*, Vol.25, No.1, February 1992.

Hamel, G. and Prahalad, C.K., "Corporate imagination and expeditionary marketing", *Harvard Business Review*, July-August 1991.

Hamel, G. and Prahalad, C.K., "Strategy as stretch and leverage", *Harvard Business Review*, March-April, 1993.

Harrigan, Kathyrn Rudie, "Joint ventures and competitive strategy", *Strategic Management Journal*, Vol.9, 1988.

Haspeslagh, P. and Jemison, D., *Managing acquisitions: creating value through corporate renewal*, Free Press, New York, 1991.

Haynes, W., "Organisational change for competitive advantage", *Business Council Bulletin*, May 1993.

Kanter, R., "How to compete", *Harvard Business Review*, July-August 1990.

Kanter, R., "Becoming PALS: pooling, allying and linking across companies", *Academy of Management Executive*, Vol.3, 1989.

Keen, P.W., *Competing in time*, Ballinger Publishing Company, Cambridge, Mass., 1987.

Lei, David and Slocum, John W. Jr., "Global strategic alliances: payoffs and pitfalls", *Organisational Dynamics*, Winter 1991.

Lewis, J.D., *Partnerships for profit: structuring and managing strategic alliances*, Free Press, New York, 1990.

Lynch, Robert Porter, "Building alliances to penetrate European markets", *The Journal of Business Strategy*, March-April 1990.

Ohmae, Kenichi, *Triad power: the coming shape of global competition*, Free Press, New York, 1985.

Pettersson, M., "'Continual improvement' for competitive advantage", *Industrial Management & Data Systems* (U.K.), No.1, 1990.

Prahalad, C.K. and Hamel, Gary, "The core competence of the corporation", *Harvard Business Review,* May-June 1990.

Powell, W., "Hybrid organisational arrangements: new form or transformational development?", *California Management Review*, Fall 1987.

Roos, J. and von Krogh, G., "Figuring out your competence configuration", *European Management Journal*, Vol.10, No.4, December 1992.

Spendolini, Michael J., *The benchmarking book,* AMACOM, New York, 1992.

Stalk, George, Jr., "Time - the next source of competitive advantage", *Quality Progress*, Vol.22, No.6, June 1989.

Stalk, G. and Hout, Thomas M., "Competing against time", *Research-Technology Management*, Vol.33, No.2, March/April, 1990.

Stalk, G. and Hout, T.M., *Competing against time: how time-based competition is reshaping global markets*, Free Press, New York, 1990.

Sutton, John R., "New cost management tools offer competitive advantage", *Industrial Engineering*, Vol.23, No.9, Sep.1991.

Weimer, G., Knill, B. Manji, J. and Beckert, B., "Compressing time-to-market: today's competitive edge", *Material Handling Engineering*, Vol.47, No.4, April 1992.

Wysocki, Bernard, Jr., "Global reach: cross-border alliances become favorite way to crack new markets", *The Wall Street Journal*, March 26, 1990.

Zachary, G. Pascal, "Blurred borders: industries find growth of digital electronics brings in competitors", *The Wall Street Journal*, February 18, 1992.

Chapter 6: The Battlefield of the Marketplace: Specific Weapons of War

Aaker, D.A., *Managing brand equity: capitalizing on the value of a brand name*, Free Press, New York, 1991.

Angelmar, R., "Product innovation: a tool for competitive advantage", *European Journal of Operational Research* (Netherlands), Vol.47, No.2, 25 July, 1990.

Bemowski, K., The benchmarking bandwagon", *Quality Progress*, January 1991.

Berry, L. and Parasuraman, A., *Marketing Services: Competing Through Quality*, Free Press, New York, 1991.

Bessant, J. and Haywood, B., "Flexible Manufacturing in Europe", *European Management Journal*, Vol.6, No.2, 1988.

Broderick, R. and Boudreau, J.W., "Human resource management, information technology, and the competitive edge", *Academy of Management Excellence*, Vol.6, No.2, May 1992.

Camp, Robert, *Benchmarking: The Search for Industry Best-Practices That Lead to Superior Performance*, Quality Resources, White Plains, N.Y., 1989.

Cherkasky, Stanley M., "Total quality for a sustainable competitive advantage", *Quality*, Vol.31, No. 8, August 1992.

Christopher, Payne and Ballantyne, *Relationship Marketing: Bringing Quality, Customer Service and Marketing Together*, Heinemann, London, 1991.

Collier, J.C., "A competitive edge through TQM", *Quality*, Vol.31, No.8, August 1992.

Coyne, W., "Innovation as a competitive advantage", *Hospitals*, Vol.64, No.10, May 20, 1990.

Cypress, H.L., "Seamless distribution gives competitive edge", *Purchasing World*, Vol.34, No.5, May 1990.

Dallaire, Rene M., "Data-based marketing for competitive advantage", *Information Strategy: The Executive's Journal*, Vol.8, No.3, Spring 1992.

Dapiran, Peter, "Benetton: global logistics in action", *Asia Pacific International Journal of Business Logistics*, Vol.5, No.3, 1992.

Drucker, Peter, "The emerging theory of manufacturing", *Harvard Business Review*, May-June 1990.

Earl, M. (ed.), *Information management: the strategic dimension*, Clarendon Press, Oxford, 1988.

Easterby-Smith, M., "Creating a learning organisation", *Personnel Review*, Vol.19, No.5.

Feigenbaum, A.V., "Quality: our new competitive edge", *Executive Excellence*, Vol.9., No.5, May 1992.

Fried, Louis and Johnson, Richard, "Gaining the technology advantage: planning for the competitive use of IT", *Journal of Information Systems Management*, Vol.8, No.4, Fall 1991.

Fuller, J.B., O'Connor, J. and Rawlinson, R., "Tailored logistics: the next advantage", *Harvard Business Review*, May-June 1993.

Furash, E.E., "Gaining a competitive edge through delivery systems", *Bankers Magazine*, Vol.173, No.4, July/August 1990.

Garvin, D.A., "How the Baldridge Award really works", *Harvard Business Review*, November-December, 1991.

Garvin, D.A., *Managing quality: the strategic and competitive edge*, Free Press New York, 1989.

Gitlow, H. and Gitlow, S., *The Deming Guide to Quality and Competitiveness*, Prentice-Hall, Englewood Cliffs, 1987.

Ghoshal, S. and Sek Ki Kim, "Building effective intelligence systems for competitive advantage", *Sloan Management Review*, Fall 1986.

Goldhar, J.D., Jelinek, M. and Schlie, T.W., "Competitive advantage in manufacturing through information technology", *International Journal of Technology Management (Switzerland)*, 1991.

Gupta, D. and Buzacott, J., "A Framework for Understanding Flexibility of Manufacturing Systems", *Journal of Manufacturing Systems*, Vol.8, No.2, 1990.

Heskett, J. and Hart, W., *Service breakthroughs: changing the rules of the game*, Free Press, New York, 1990.

Humphreys, M., "Logistics management: a competitive edge", *Production and Inventory Management Review & APICS News*, November 1988.

Inglis, Paul F., "Quality logistics: a key competitive advantage", *Canadian Business Review*, Vol.19, No.2, Summer 1992.

James, D. and Gottliebsen, R., "World-best practice: a matter of survival", *Business Review Weekly*, January 17, 1992.

Kim, D.H., "Toward learning organisations: integrated total quality control and systems thinking", *Sloan School of Management*, October 1990.

Kotter. J.P., *The leadership factor*, Free Press, New York, 1988.

Lengnik-Hall, Cynthia A., "Innovation and competitive advantage: what we know and what we need to learn", *Journal of Management*, Vol.18, No.2, June 1992.

Lodge, C., "Total quality focus gives container maker competitive edge", *Plastics World*, Vol.50, No.8, June 1990.

Morgan, "Drastic changes for management", *Business Month*, March, 1989.

Morton, M.S., *Corporations of the 1990s: information technology and organisational transformations*, Oxford University Press, New York, 1991.

Peterson, R., "Creating competitive advantage through information technology", *Trustee*, Vol.43, No.11, November 1990.

Porras, J. and Silvers, R., "Organisational development and transformation", *Annual Reviews*, 1991.

Porter, M. and Miller, V., "How information gives you competitive advantage", *Harvard Business Review*, 63(4).

Pryor, L.S., "Benchmarking: a self-improvement strategy", *The Journal of Business Strategy*, November-December 1989.

Ramsover, Reagan M., "Competitive advantage with information technology", *Baylor Business Review*, Vol.9, Fall 1991.

Senge, Peter, *The fifth discipline: the art and practice of the learning organisation*, Doubleday/Currency, London, 1990.

Senge, Peter, "The learning organisation made plain", *Training & Development*, October 1991.

Senker, Jacqueline and Senker, Peter, "Gaining competitive advantage from information technology", *Journal of General Management*, Vol.17, No.3, Spring 1992.

Senn, James A., "The myths of strategic systems: what defines true competitive advantage", *Information Systems Management*, Vol.9, No.3, Summer 1992.

Serrano, Ron, "After TQM: turning quality into a competitive advantage", *Telephone Engineer and Management*, Supplement, January 15, 1992.

Shetty, Y.K., "Product quality and competitive strategy", *Business Horizons*, 30, May-June 1987, pp.46-52.

Skinner, Wickham, "The shareholder's delight: companies that achieve competitive advantage from process innovation", *International Journal of Technology Management*, Vol.7, No.1-3, 1992.

Stalk, G., Evans, P. and Shulman, L., "Competing on capabilities: the new rules of corporate strategy", *Harvard Business Review*, March-April 1992.

Stata, R., "Organisational learning: the key to management innovation", *Sloan Management Review*, Spring 1989.

Sutton, H., "Keeping Tabs on the Competition", *Marketing Communications*, Vol.14, January 1989.

Turner, Paul, "Using information to enhance competitive advantage: the marketing options", *European Journal of Marketing*, Vol.25, No.6, 1991.

Vandore, J., "The missing 'P' in the marketing mix is you", *Marketing*, November 1992.

Vaziri, H.K., "Using competitive benchmarking to set goals", *Quality Progress*, October 1992.

Vives, X., "Information and competitive advantage", *International Journal of Industrial Organisation* (Netherlands), Vol.8, No.1, April 1990.

Walsworth, Brenda, "Applying technology for competitive advantage", *Retail Control*, Vol.59, Issue 6, July/August, 1991.

West, K., "Quality: the ultimate competitive advantage", *Accountancy,* Vol.108, Issue 1176, August 1991.

Zeithmal, D., *Delivering quality service: balancing customer perceptions and expectations*, Kent Pub. Co., London, 1990.

Zuboff, S., *In the age of the smart machine: the future of work and power*, Basic Books, New York, 1988.

Chapter 7: The Ability to Compete

Day, George S. and Wensley, Robin, "Assessing advantage: a framework for diagnosing competitive advantage", *Journal of Marketing*, 52, No.2, April 1988.

Shapiro, Benson P., "What the hell is 'market oriented'?", *Harvard Business Review*, November-December, 1988.